CONTENTS

**Suggested for
the week of:**

Unit 25: Jesus' Early Ministry

Unit 26: Jesus Performed Miracles

Unit 27: Jesus Preached

Special Features

Bible Study at a Glance

Start here

Leader Bible study

Familiarize yourself with the context of the Bible story and how it relates to God's plan of redemption.

Session Starters

Activity Page

Small Group Opening

Use opening activities and session starters to introduce the day's Bible story.

Key Passage

Timeline Map

Large Group Leader

This 30-minute teaching time allows you to watch or tell the Bible story. Large group elements reinforce the Bible story and Christ Connection.

Big Picture Question

Review

Sing

The Gospel: God's Plan for Me

Discussion Starter

Say what?
Use the suggested "Leader" and "Say" dialogue to easily move between segments.

Suggested times
The times provided allow you to complete the session plan in an hour and fifteen minutes. Lengthen or shorten the session as needed.

Make it fit

Customize the session plan to fit the needs of your church or classroom.

1 room

1) Use the Small Group Opening to welcome kids to Bible Study. Kids may work the activity page and/or complete an activity together.
2) Transition to an area within your classroom that can be designated as the Large Group Bible story area. Watch the Bible story video or tell the Bible story. Incorporate any large group elements that fit your space and your time constraints.
3) Regroup to the Small Group area by using a countdown video or gather around a table as you review the key passage and practice Bible skills.

1 or more rooms

1) Use the Small Group Opening to welcome kids to Bible Study. Kids may work the activity page and/or complete an activity together.
2) Use the countdown video or other other transition signal as you move your small group to join the other small groups in the Large Group area. Watch the Bible story video or tell the Bible story. Incorporate any large group elements that fit your space and your time constraints.
3) Regroup to the Small Group rooms where you will reinforce what the kids learned from the Large Group Leader, review the key passage, and practice Bible skills.

Journal

Key Passage Activity

Bible Story Review & Bible Skills

Activities

Small Group Leader

Review the Bible story, build Bible skills, engage in activity options, and more!

Finish here

Check out our tips and resources for an additional hour in the Worship Guide!

Unit 25: JESUS' EARLY MINISTRY

Big Picture Questions

Session 1:
Why do we need to be born again? Because of sin we are spiritually dead, but Jesus came to give us new life.

Session 2:
Where did Jesus come from? God sent Jesus to earth from heaven.

Session 3:
What does Jesus offer? Jesus offers eternal life.

Session 4:
What is the good news about Jesus? Jesus died for our sins.

Unit 25: JESUS' EARLY MINISTRY

Unit Description: Jesus began His ministry on earth and revealed that He is the promised Messiah—the One God promised who would bring salvation to the world.

Unit Key Passage:
John 3:16-17

Unit Christ Connection:
Jesus was revealed as the fulfillment of Scripture, the promised Savior.

Session 1:
Jesus Met Nicodemus
John 3:1-21

Session 2:
Jesus and John the Baptist
John 3:22-36

Session 3:
Jesus Met a Samaritan Woman
John 4:1-26

Session 4:
Rejection at Nazareth
Luke 4:16-30

Leader BIBLE STUDY

Jesus' ministry had begun. His first miracle was at a wedding in Cana, turning water into wine. He cleansed the temple in Jerusalem and performed signs, and "many trusted in His name" (John 2:23). Jesus likely spent a large part of His day teaching. When the day was done, He spent time alone or with His disciples. One night, however, a man named Nicodemus approached Jesus.

Nicodemus was a Pharisee and a ruler of the Jews; that is, he was a religious leader who taught God's law, and he was a member of the Sanhedrin—a Jewish governing body. Nicodemus was part of an exclusive group of religious elite who appeared to be moral men. He held to the belief that if a person was a law-abiding Jew, then he would be accepted by God. Jesus gave Nicodemus a lesson that would turn his belief system on its head.

Jesus was a carpenter (Mark 6:3), so the religious teachers likely assumed He didn't know theology. But they had seen Jesus' miraculous signs in Jerusalem. Nicodemus, a representative of the teachers, had to conclude, "You are a teacher come from God" (John 3:2).

Nicodemus initiated the conversation, but Jesus chose the subject. His words perplexed Nicodemus: "Unless someone is born again, he cannot see the kingdom of God" (John 3:3). Jesus explained that spiritual birth is not unlike physical birth in that a person cannot do it himself. It is something that happens to him.

Jesus reminded Nicodemus of an Old Testament account, the disobedient Israelites and the bronze snake. The Israelites could not help themselves, but when they trusted in God and looked to the bronze snake lifted up on the pole, they were healed. (Num. 21:4-9)

Every person is born a sinner—spiritually dead and alienated from God. It is by God's Spirit—not our own effort—that we are born again. We look to Christ and His finished work on the cross for our salvation.

Older Kids BIBLE STUDY OVERVIEW

Session Title: Jesus Met Nicodemus
Bible Passage: John 3:1-21
Big Picture Question: Why do we need to be born again? Because of sin we are spiritually dead, but Jesus came to give us new life.
Key Passage: John 3:16-17
Unit Christ Connection: Jesus was revealed as the fulfillment of Scripture, the promised Savior.

Small Group Opening

Large Group Leader

Small Group Leader

The BIBLE STORY

Jesus Met Nicodemus
John 3:1-21

Jesus had traveled to Jerusalem for the Passover Festival. **One night, a man came to see Jesus.** The man's name was Nicodemus (NIK uh DEE muhs). Nicodemus was a Pharisee. That means he was a religious man. He studied and taught God's law, and he tried very hard to obey the law. Nicodemus had heard about Jesus, and he wanted to know more.

"Rabbi (RAB igh)**," he said, "we know that You have come from God. You are a teacher, and no one could do the miracles You do unless God is with him."**

Nicodemus was right. Jesus *was* a teacher, and He was very good at teaching. Jesus *had* come from heaven, and God *was* with Him.

Jesus said, "I tell you: Unless someone is born again, he cannot see the kingdom of God."

Now Nicodemus was very confused. He thought that keeping all God's laws was how a person got into heaven. Besides, what Jesus said didn't make any sense! **"How can anyone be born when he is old?" Nicodemus asked Jesus.**

Jesus said, "I tell you: A man cannot enter God's kingdom unless he is born of water and the Spirit. Whatever is born of the flesh is flesh, and whatever is born of the Spirit is spirit." That means that when a baby is born, he gets physical life from his parents. Physical life doesn't last forever. But the Spirit gives people spiritual life so they can live with God forever.

Jesus said, "Don't be surprised I told you that you must be born again." Nicodemus still didn't understand. "How is this possible?" he asked.

"You are a teacher in Israel, and you don't understand what I'm saying?" Jesus replied. "This is the truth: We talk about what we know, and we tell others about what we have seen. But you don't believe what I'm telling you! When I tell you about things I've seen on earth, and you don't believe me, how will you believe what I say about the things I've seen in heaven?

"No one has ever gone up into heaven, except the Son of Man. He came down from heaven. **Do you remember how Moses raised up the bronze snake in the wilderness? Everyone who looked at it was healed. Like that, the Son of Man will be raised up, so that everyone who believes in Him will have eternal life.**"

Then Jesus told Nicodemus about God's great plan. Jesus said, "God loved the world so much that He sent His One and Only Son to save the world. Everyone who believes in Him will not perish but will have eternal life. God didn't send His Son to declare the world guilty, but to save the world. Anyone who believes in Him is found not guilty, but anyone who does not believe in Him is guilty already."

Christ Connection: Without Jesus, we are spiritually dead. Sin separates us from God. When people believe in Christ and are "born again," they receive new life and become God's children. Jesus offers new life to those who trust in Him for salvation.

Small Group OPENING

Session Title: Jesus Met Nicodemus
Bible Passage: John 3:1-21
Big Picture Question: Why do we need to be born again? Because of sin we are spiritually dead, but Jesus came to give us new life.
Key Passage: John 3:16-17
Unit Christ Connection: Jesus was revealed as the fulfillment of Scripture, the promised Savior.

Welcome time

Greet each kid as he or she arrives. Use this time to collect the offering, fill out attendance sheets, and help new kids connect to your group. Ask each kid to share any details she knows about her birth—what time of day it was, what day of the week it was, where she was born, and so forth.

Activity page (5 minutes)

- "Rephrase It" activity page, 1 per kid
- pencils

Challenge kids to list *re-* words on the "Rephrase It" activity page. Tell kids that the prefix *re-* means "again."

Say • In today's Bible story, Jesus told a man that he needed to do something again. Do you know what that was?

Invite a kid to read John 3:3 aloud. Prompt kids to determine which *re-* word means "born again." (*reborn*)

Session starter (10 minutes)

- blindfolds, 3
- shoes with laces, 3
- Bibles
- matching socks, 6 pairs

Option 1: In the dark

Choose three volunteers to compete. Blindfold each volunteer. Announce a task for the volunteers to perform. Allow them to complete one or more of the suggested tasks. Then choose three new volunteers to try.

1. Give each kid an untied shoe. Challenge kids to tie the shoelaces without looking. Bonus: Unlace the shoes and require kids to lace them before they tie them.

2. Give each kid a Bible. Challenge kids to turn to John 3. Bonus: Instruct kids to point to verse 16.

3. Give each kid two pairs of matching socks. Challenge kids to pair the matching socks. Bonus: Turn a few of the socks inside out and instruct kids to turn all of the socks right-side out.

Say • Good job, everyone! These were all hard to do in the dark. In our Bible story today, a man named Nicodemus came to Jesus at night. We'll find out how Nicodemus was, in a way, living his life in the dark.

Option 2: Into the light

• box or gift bag
• 6 to 8 common household items: highlighting marker, unsharpened pencil, crayon, block eraser, magnet, ball of foil, spoon, ruler, and so forth

Place several common items in a gift bag or box. Choose a volunteer to stand in front of the group. Hold the bag behind her back and challenge her to pull a specific item from the bag without looking. Encourage the volunteer to feel the items to select the correct one. When she chooses the item, she should hold it up to see if she is correct. Place the item back in the bag and choose another volunteer to take a turn.

Once kids have displayed several of the items, play again by handing the volunteer an item behind her back. She should describe to the group how the item feels (long, short, round, smooth, and so forth) and let the group identify it.

Say • Today we are going to hear a Bible story about a man named Nicodemus. Nicodemus talked to Jesus at night. He did not know the truth about God. Jesus came to tell people the truth about God and to bring them into the light.

Transition to large group

Jesus' Early Ministry

Large Group LEADER

Session Title: Jesus Met Nicodemus
Bible Passage: John 3:1-21
Big Picture Question: Why do we need to be born again? Because of sin we are spiritually dead, but Jesus came to give us new life.
Key Passage: John 3:16-17
Unit Christ Connection: Jesus was revealed as the fulfillment of Scripture, the promised Savior.

• room decorations

Tip: Select decorations that fit your ministry and budget.

Suggested Theme Decorating Ideas: Simulate a theme park by hanging a large piece of blue paper or a tablecloth as a sky backdrop. Draw some large and small hills to outline a roller coaster track. Position small artificial plants in the foreground or use green paper to represent bushes and grass. Hang a colorful pennant banner and a sign that says "Welcome" or "Entrance."

Countdown

• countdown video

Show the countdown video as your kids arrive, and set it to end as large group time begins.

Introduce the session (2 minutes)

• leader attire
• map

[Large Group Leader enters wearing a name tag, a hat or visor, and a button that says "Ask Me!" Leader is also carrying a map.]

Leader • Hello there! I'm [*your name*]. Nice to meet you! I'm so glad you arrived safely at the Early Days Theme Park! I'll be your chaperone, which is a fancy way of saying I'll be your guide. If you have any questions, ask me. [*Closely examine a map.*]

Each week, we're going on a new adventure in the New Testament. Is everybody ready? Then let's go!

Timeline map (2 minutes)

• Timeline Map

Display the timeline map where kids can see it. As you introduce the Bible story, point to it on the timeline map.

Leader •One of the things I love about working at an amusement park is that I get to meet so many people! Do you like meeting new people? Maybe meeting new people makes you a little nervous, but sometimes new acquaintances turn out to be really great friends. Today we're going to hear a story about a man who met Jesus. Let's see … here it is. Our Bible story is called "Jesus Met Nicodemus."

Cool. I wonder what Nicodemus and Jesus talked about when they met. Do you have any ideas? Well, we will find out very soon.

Big picture question (1 minute)

Leader •Oh, I almost forgot. I have a special assignment for you. We have a big picture question that I don't know the answer to. Will you listen to the Bible story to help me find the answer? Today's question is, **Why do we need to be born again?**

Tell the Bible story (10 minutes)

• "Jesus Met Nicodemus" video
• Bibles, 1 per kid
• Bible Story Picture Slide or Poster
• Big Picture Question Slide or Poster

Open your Bible to John 3:1-21 and tell the Bible story in your own words, or show the Bible story video "Jesus Met Nicodemus."

Leader •Nicodemus was a Pharisee. He tried hard to obey God's laws. Many Pharisees thought that a person could get to heaven by being good. Is that how we get to heaven? By obeying God and doing good things? No. God wants us to obey Him, but the Bible says everyone sins. (Rom. 3:23) If we had to obey God perfectly to go to heaven, no one would ever get to heaven!

Tip: A Bible story script is provided at the beginning of every session. You may use it to guide you as you prepare to teach the Bible story in your own words. For a shorter version of the Bible story, read only the bolded text.

Jesus told Nicodemus that a person must be born again to go to heaven. Jesus wasn't talking about being born again physically like babies are born; He meant that people have to be born again spiritually. Without Jesus, we are spiritually dead. We are separated from God.

Why do we need to be born again? Because of sin we are spiritually dead, but Jesus came to give us new life. Say that with me. *Why do we need to be born again? Because of sin we are spiritually dead, but Jesus came to give us new life.*

Jesus reminded Nicodemus of something that happened in the Old Testament. [*See Num. 21:4-9.*] When God's people were in the wilderness, they complained and disobeyed God. God sent poisonous snakes that bit the people, and many Israelites died. The people could not do anything to save themselves. Then God told Moses to make a bronze snake and put it on a pole. Anyone who was bitten could look at the bronze snake and be healed.

That bronze snake reminds us of Jesus. Jesus was lifted up on the cross. He died for our sins and was raised from the dead. We can't do anything to save ourselves, but we can look to Jesus for salvation. Jesus obeyed God perfectly for us. Without Jesus, we are spiritually dead. Sin separates us from God. When people believe in Christ and are "born again," they receive new life and become God's children. Jesus offers new life to those who trust in Him for salvation.

God's great plan for the world is to save sinners. Jesus told Nicodemus about this plan.

The Gospel: God's Plan for Me (optional)

· Bible

Using Scripture and the guide provided, explain to boys and girls how to become a Christian. Tell kids how they

can respond, and provide counselors to speak with each kid individually. Guide counselors to use open-ended questions to allow kids to determine the direction of the conversation.

Encourage boys and girls to ask their parents, small group leaders, or other adults any questions they may have about becoming a Christian.

Key passage (5 minutes)

- Key Passage Slide or Poster
- "God So Loved" song

Leader • Our key passage is from the Book of John, one of the four Gospels. Can anyone tell me what the Gospels are about? (*Jesus' life, death, and resurrection*)

Guide kids to find John 3:16-17 in their Bibles. Remind them that the Book of John is the fourth book in the New Testament. Choose a volunteer to read the passage aloud.

Leader • Jesus said these words to Nicodemus when He met him at night. Jesus told Nicodemus about God's plan for the world. God sent Jesus to die on the cross to take the punishment for sin. Sin separates people from God, but whoever believes in Jesus has eternal life. Believers will live with God forever in heaven.

Lead the group to repeat the entire key passage together. Sing "God So Loved."

Discussion starter video (5 minutes)

- "Unit 25 Session 1" discussion starter video

Leader • Nicodemus was surprised by what Jesus said about how a person enters God's kingdom. Nicodemus thought that people got to heaven by obeying God's law perfectly. What do you think? Let's watch this video.

Show the "Unit 25 Session 1" video.

Leader • Did any of these kids know the right answer?

Invite kids to respond. Remind them that the Bible says we can't earn our way to heaven. (See Eph. 2:8-9; Acts 16:31.) We can trust in Jesus for salvation.

Sing (3 minutes)

• "The Only Name (Yours Will Be)" song

Leader • Nicodemus thought that a person got to heaven by obeying God's law perfectly. The problem is that we all sin. No one obeys God's law perfectly. No one except Jesus. Sin makes us spiritually dead, but we can look to Jesus for new life. And there's nothing we can do to earn it! Salvation is a free gift from God!

That's worth singing about. Will you sing our theme song with me? It's about Jesus and how His name is the most important name. The Bible says that Jesus is worthy of our worship because He is Lord. [*See Phil. 2:9-11.*]
Lead boys and girls to sing "The Only Name (Yours Will Be)."

Prayer (2 minutes)

Leader • Wow! This is great. I've learned so much, and we are just getting started. Who knew Jesus' early ministry was full of so much adventure? Will you come back next week? Oh, wonderful!

Now, one more time: ***Why do we need to be born again? Because of sin we are spiritually dead, but Jesus came to give us new life.*** Great job. Before you go to your small groups, I am going to pray.
Close in prayer. Thank God for showing His love to the world by sending Jesus, His One and Only Son. Confess that we all deserve to be punished for our sin, but praise God for His gift of eternal life. Pray that kids would believe in Jesus as Lord and Savior.

Dismiss to small groups

The Gospel: God's Plan for Me

Ask kids if they have ever heard the word *gospel*. Clarify that the word *gospel* means "good news." It is the message about Christ, the kingdom of God, and salvation. Use the following guide to share the gospel with kids.

God rules. Explain to kids that the Bible tells us God created everything, and He is in charge of everything. Invite a volunteer to read Genesis 1:1 from the Bible. Read Revelation 4:11 or Colossians 1:16-17 aloud and explain what these verses mean.

We sinned. Tell kids that since the time of Adam and Eve, everyone has chosen to disobey God. (Romans 3:23) The Bible calls this sin. Because God is holy, God cannot be around sin. Sin separates us from God and deserves God's punishment of death. (Romans 6:23)

God provided. Choose a child to read John 3:16 aloud. Say that God sent His Son, Jesus, the perfect solution to our sin problem, to rescue us from the punishment we deserve. It's something we, as sinners, could never earn on our own. Jesus alone saves us. Read and explain Ephesians 2:8-9.

Jesus gives. Share with kids that Jesus lived a perfect life, died on the cross for our sins, and rose again. Because Jesus gave up His life for us, we can be welcomed into God's family for eternity. This is the best gift ever! Read Romans 5:8; 2 Corinthians 5:21; or 1 Peter 3:18.

We respond. Tell kids that they can respond to Jesus. Read Romans 10:9-10,13. Review these aspects of our response: Believe in your heart that Jesus alone saves you through what He's already done on the cross. Repent, turning from self and sin to Jesus. Tell God and others that your faith is in Jesus.

Offer to talk with any child who is interested in responding to Jesus.

Small Group LEADER

Session Title: Jesus Met Nicodemus
Bible Passage: John 3:1-21
Big Picture Question: Why do we need to be born again? Because of sin we are spiritually dead, but Jesus came to give us new life.
Key Passage: John 3:16-17
Unit Christ Connection: Jesus was revealed as the fulfillment of Scripture, the promised Savior.

Key passage activity (5 minutes)

- Key Passage Poster
- craft sticks
- marker

Write phrases of the key passage on separate craft sticks. Mix them up and scatter them on the floor or a table. Challenge kids to rearrange the sticks to put the verses in order. Kids may refer to the key passage poster if necessary.

When kids finish, lead them to recite the passage together. Then mix up the sticks and play again. As kids learn the passage, cover the key passage poster or take away one or two of the sticks. Kids should say the key passage together, reciting any missing phrases from memory.

Say • Great job, everyone! Jesus said these words to Nicodemus. These words tell us the gospel—the good news about Jesus. God sent Jesus into the world to save sinners.

Bible story review & Bible skills (10 minutes)

- Bibles, 1 per kid
- Small Group Visual Pack
- marker
- index cards

Help kids find John 3:1-21 in their Bibles. Explain that the Book of John is one of the four Gospels. The Gospels tell about Jesus' life, death, and resurrection. Review the Bible story in your own words or retell the story using the bolded portions of the Bible story script.

Write the numbers *1–8* on separate index cards. On the back of each index card, write a point value. Position the cards number-side up on the floor or a table. Form two groups. Allow groups to take turns choosing a numbered card. Read the corresponding question. If a team answers correctly, it earns the indicated number of points. If a team is wrong, give the other team a chance to answer.

1. What was Nicodemus's job? (*He was a Pharisee, a ruler of the Jews; John 3:1*)
2. When did Nicodemus go to see Jesus? (*at night, John 3:2*)
3. What did Jesus say has to happen for someone to see God's kingdom? (*He must be born again, John 3:3*)
4. Did Nicodemus understand what Jesus said? (*No; John 3:4,9*)
5. How does Jesus know what heaven is like? (*Jesus came from heaven, John 3:11-13*)
6. How did God show His love to the world? (*He gave His One and Only Son, so that everyone who believes in Him will not perish but have eternal life; John 3:16*)
7. Why did God send His Son into the world? (*so that the world might be saved through Him, John 3:17*)
8. **Why do we need to be born again? Because of sin we are spiritually dead, but Jesus came to give us new life.**

If you choose to review with boys and girls how to become a Christian, explain that kids are welcome to speak with you or another teacher if they have questions.

- **God rules.** God created and is in charge of everything. (Gen. 1:1; Rev. 4:11; Col. 1:16-17)
- **We sinned.** Since Adam and Eve, everyone has chosen to disobey God. (Rom. 3:23; 6:23)
- **God provided.** God sent His Son, Jesus, to rescue

us from the punishment we deserve. (John 3:16; Eph. 2:8-9)

- **Jesus gives.** Jesus lived a perfect life, died on the cross for our sins, and rose again so we can be welcomed into God's family. (Rom. 5:8; 2 Cor. 5:21; 1 Pet. 3:18)
- **We respond.** Believe that Jesus alone saves you. Repent. Tell God that your faith is in Jesus. (Rom. 10:9-10,13)

Activity choice (10 minutes)

Option 1: What's in the bag?

Put a small toy or candy in a gift bag. Give each kid a piece of paper and a marker. Challenge each kid to draw a picture of what she thinks is in the bag.

After a few minutes, invite each kid to share her guess. Play several rounds, swapping out what is inside the bag. You may choose to give each kid a gift—a small toy or piece of candy—to conclude the game.

- gift bag
- small toys or candies
- paper
- markers
- Allergy Alert (optional)

Say • *Why do we need to be born again? Because of sin we are spiritually dead, but Jesus came to give us new life.*

- Jesus told Nicodemus about God's great plan to save sinners. Jesus came to give eternal life to people who believe in Him. We cannot do anything to earn our way to heaven; salvation is a free gift from God.

- disposable bowl
- spoon
- 1 cup water
- 1½–2 cups cornstarch
- paper towels or wet wipes
- food color (optional)
- Allergy Alert (enhanced CD)

Option 2: Make *oobleck*

Demonstrate how to make *oobleck*, a substance that acts like both a solid and a liquid. First, pour 1 cup of water into a disposable bowl. Gradually add 1½ cups cornstarch. Stir thoroughly or mix with your hands. Adjust the consistency of the oobleck by adding more water or cornstarch. Show

Tip: Use warm water to clean oobleck from your hands or surfaces. Store in an airtight container or ziplock bag. Dispose of mixture in a trash can rather than a sink.

kids how the oobleck reacts to touch by slowly pulling your fingers through it. The oobleck will flow and drip like a liquid. Poke or punch the oobleck. Applying pressure to the mixture will make it will feel hard like a solid.

If you wish, allow kids to experiment with the oobleck. Invite them to knead it, roll it, or pour it. Provide paper towels or wet wipes for cleanup.

Remind kids that Jesus told Nicodemus that a person has to be born again to enter God's kingdom.

Say • *Why do we need to be born again? Without Jesus, we are spiritually dead.*

• Without Jesus, we are spiritually dead. Our hearts are hard, and we love sin more than we love God. But God can soften people's hearts. Jesus offers new life to those who trust in Him for salvation.

Journal and prayer (5 minutes)

• pencils
• journals
• Bibles
• Journal Page, 1 per kid (enhanced CD)
• "Unlikely Pairs" activity page, 1 per kid

Lead kids to list on their journal pages things they can do on their own and things they need others to do for them. For example: "I can make my bed. I need someone else to drive me to school." Point out that being born again is not something we can do for ourselves, but when we believe in Jesus, God gives us eternal life.

Say • *Why do we need to be born again? Because of sin we are spiritually dead, but Jesus came to give us new life.*

Invite kids to share prayer requests. Close the group in prayer, thanking Jesus for obeying God perfectly and dying on the cross so we can have eternal life.

As time allows, lead kids to complete the activity page "Unlikely Pairs."

Leader BIBLE STUDY

Following His encounter with Nicodemus, Jesus went with His disciples into the countryside of Judea. Jesus oversaw His disciples as they baptized people. (Jesus Himself did not baptize. See John 4:2.) At the same time, people came to John, and he was baptizing them. These baptisms were an outward sign of cleansing for people who had repented from their sins.

Some of John's disciples came to John. They had noticed that the man John had reluctantly baptized was now baptizing others. Perhaps they felt the need to defend John's ministry, but John explained the purpose God had for his life. John had been chosen by God long before he was born to be a forerunner—one who prepares the way. (See Mal. 3:1; Isa. 40:3.)

John the Baptist understood who he was and who Jesus is. Consider these comparisons as John explained that Jesus was greater than John.

First, who were they? John was clear: "I am not the Messiah" (John 3:28). John was not the bridegroom, but the groom's friend. Jesus is the bridegroom. (John 3:29)

Where did they come from? John was from the earth, and he belonged to the earth. Jesus comes from above and is above all. (John 3:31)

Next, what did they do? John said, "He must increase, but I must decrease." As the predecessor, John was a witness to the Light. (John 1:7-8) He was a voice in the wilderness, and Jesus is the Word. (John 1:14,23) John baptized with water, but Jesus baptized with the Spirit. (John 1:33)

Finally, why were they here? John went before Jesus and rejoiced with Him. (John 3:28-29) Jesus came to give eternal life. (John 3:36)

In the scope of God's plan of salvation, it was time for John to step aside for Jesus to do His work on earth. Jesus' earthly ministry had begun, and He would obediently do God's will to bring salvation to sinners.

Older Kids BIBLE STUDY OVERVIEW

Session Title: Jesus and John the Baptist
Bible Passage: John 3:22-36
Big Picture Question: Where did Jesus come from? God sent Jesus to earth from heaven.
Key Passage: John 3:16-17
Unit Christ Connection: Jesus was revealed as the fulfillment of Scripture, the promised Savior.

Small Group Opening

Large Group Leader

Small Group Leader

The BIBLE STORY

Jesus and John the Baptist
John 3:22-36

Jesus and His disciples left Jerusalem, and they **went out into the countryside.** Jesus spent time with His disciples. **People came to them, and Jesus taught the people, and the people were baptized.**

Nearby, John the Baptist was baptizing people too. Some of the people who followed John got into an argument. They went to John to ask him a question.

"Teacher," they said, **"remember the man you talked about, the One who was with you on the other side of the Jordan River? He is baptizing people, and people are starting to follow Him."**

John answered them, "A person can only receive what God gives him. **You heard me say that I am not the Messiah. I am the messenger who goes before Him to announce that He is coming."**

John tried to explain by talking about a wedding. When two people get married, **the man who marries the bride is the groom. His friend stands with him at the wedding, and he is happy to be there** and hear the groom's voice. **This was how John felt—like a groom's friend— because he was happy that Jesus, the Messiah, had come.**

John also knew that a wedding is the groom's special day; the groom's friend should not make it about himself. John said about Jesus, "He must become greater, and I must become less."

Then John explained why Jesus was more important than himself. John was from the earth, and he could only talk about things on earth. Jesus—the One who comes from heaven—talked about things in heaven because He had seen them! Still, no one believed what Jesus said.

John said, "Whoever believes Jesus knows that God tells the truth. God sent Jesus to earth, and Jesus speaks God's words."

John also said, "The Father loves the Son and has given Him power over everything. Whoever believes in the Son will have eternal life, but whoever refuses to believe in the Son will not have eternal life. He will never be able to get away from God's anger."

Christ Connection: John the Baptist had told people to get ready for Jesus, the promised Messiah. Now that Jesus was there, John's mission was complete. John the Baptist joyfully stepped aside as Jesus began His earthly ministry.

Small Group OPENING

Session Title: Jesus and John the Baptist
Bible Passage: John 3:22-36
Big Picture Question: Where did Jesus come from? God sent Jesus to earth from heaven.
Key Passage: John 3:16-17
Unit Christ Connection: Jesus was revealed as the fulfillment of Scripture, the promised Savior.

Welcome time

Greet each kid as he or she arrives. Use this time to collect the offering, fill out attendance sheets, and help new kids connect to your group.

Ask kids if any of them have ever met someone famous. Whom would kids like to meet?

Activity page (5 minutes)

- "Roller Coaster Roundup" activity page, 1 per kid
- pencils

Invite kids to work alone or in pairs on the activity page "Roller Coast Roundup." Boys and girls should take a ride on the roller coaster to collect letters along the track. Guide kids to write the letters in the boxes provided to find the name of someone in today's Bible story. (*John the Baptist*)

Say • John the Baptist had a job: to get people ready for Jesus. Now that Jesus had come, what did John the Baptist do? We will find out in today's Bible story.

Session starter (10 minutes)

Option 1: Wedding words

Direct kids to stand in a circle. Choose one kid to begin. He should say one word associated with a wedding. For example, *tuxedo* or *music*. Continue around the circle, inviting kids to take turns sharing words related to a wedding. Determine whether or not a shared word is associated with a wedding. If a kid cannot think of a word or repeats a word that has already been shared, he should sit down. Play until only one kid remains standing.

If time remains, play again with a different category, such as words associated with Jesus, words associated with baptism, or words associated with church.

Say • In our Bible story today, John the Baptist told his followers that Jesus is like a groom, and John was like the groom's friend. We'll find out more about what he meant in the large group time.

Option 2: Where are you from?

Display a world map or a map of your country, state, or city. Invite kids to point to their hometowns, or provide small stickers to mark where they are from.

- map of world, country, state, or city
- small round or star stickers (optional)

Allow kids to share about the places they marked on the map. Who has lived the farthest away? Who has always lived in your current city?

As time allows, lead kids to discuss other places they have traveled or places they would like to visit someday.

Say • Today we are going to hear a story from the Bible about Jesus and John the Baptist. John told his followers some important things about Jesus— including where Jesus came from.

Transition to large group

Large Group LEADER

Session Title: Jesus and John the Baptist
Bible Passage: John 3:22-36
Big Picture Question: Where did Jesus come from? God sent Jesus to earth from heaven.
Key Passage: John 3:16-17
Unit Christ Connection: Jesus was revealed as the fulfillment of Scripture, the promised Savior.

Countdown

• countdown video

Show the countdown video as your kids arrive, and set it to end as large group time begins.

Introduce the session (2 minutes)

• leader attire
• map

[Large Group Leader enters wearing a name tag, a hat or visor, and a button that says "Ask Me!" Leader is also carrying a map.]

Leader •You came back! I hope you're ready for today's Bible story because we're going to jump right in. First, I better see where we're going. Let's look at the timeline map.

Timeline map (2 minutes)

• Timeline Map

Use the timeline map to point out and review the previous Bible story, "Jesus Met Nicodemus."

Leader •Look at our timeline map. Does anyone remember who came to visit Jesus at night? That's right. The man's name was Nicodemus. Jesus told Nicodemus that a person has to be born again to enter God's kingdom.

Why do we need to be born again? Because of sin we are spiritually dead, but Jesus came to give us new life.

Today, we're going to hear some important things John the Baptist said about Jesus, like who Jesus is and where He came from.

Big picture question (1 minute)

Leader • That leads me to our big picture question. Our big picture question is, ***Where did Jesus come from?*** If you think you know the answer, raise your hand but don't say it aloud just yet. Listen carefully to today's Bible story to see if you are correct.

Tell the Bible story (10 minutes)

- "Jesus and John the Baptist" video
- Bibles, 1 per kid
- Bible Story Picture Slide or Poster
- Big Picture Question Slide or Poster

Open your Bible to John 3:22-36 and tell the Bible story in your own words, or show the Bible story video "Jesus and John the Baptist."

Leader • Jesus was in the countryside with His disciples. Many people came to follow Jesus and be baptized. John the Baptist had followers, too. John's followers were people who learned from him as he told people to get ready for Jesus. They noticed that people were following this man named Jesus instead of following John. What was going on?

John explained to his followers who he was and who Jesus is. John said, "I am not the Messiah." John did not want his followers to look to him for salvation; he wanted them to look to Jesus. John could not save people from their sins. His job was to announce that the Messiah—the One who has the power to save people—was coming.

John even said that Jesus was like the groom at a wedding, and John was like the groom's friend. Everyone knows the groom at a wedding is more important than the groom's friend.

John also talked about where he came from and where

Jesus came from. John said that he came from the earth. ***Where did Jesus come from? God sent Jesus to earth from heaven.*** That's our big picture question and answer. Say it with me. ***Where did Jesus come from? God sent Jesus to earth from heaven.***

John said other things about himself and Jesus. He said, "He must increase, but I must decrease." What does that mean? John meant that it was time for him to get out of the spotlight. Jesus had come, and Jesus is more important than John. John's mission of telling people to get ready for Jesus was complete, and John joyfully stepped aside as Jesus began His earthly ministry.

The Gospel: God's Plan for Me (optional)

• Bible

Using Scripture and the guide provided, explain to boys and girls how to become a Christian. Tell kids how they can respond, and provide counselors to speak with each kid individually.

Encourage boys and girls to ask their parents, small group leaders, or other adults any questions they may have about becoming a Christian.

Key passage (5 minutes)

• Key Passage Slide or Poster
• "God So Loved" song

Note: If kids already know John 3:16-17 or are quick to master it, challenge them to memorize verse 18 as well.

Leader • Let's practice our key passage, John 3:16-17. Can anyone say it from memory?

Invite kids who memorized John 3:16-17 to recite it aloud. Then guide everyone to find they key passage in the Bible.

Explain that John, who wrote the Book of John, was one of Jesus' twelve disciples. (See Matt. 4:21-22.) God used John to write His words in the Bible. Lead the kids in saying the passage together.

Leader • Remember, these are the words Jesus said to Nicodemus when He met him at night. Jesus told

Nicodemus about God's great plan for the world. This is the gospel, the good news about Jesus! God planned to give eternal life to whoever believes in Jesus—people from all nations of the world, not only the Jewish people. Though we may die a physical death, as believers we will live with God forever in heaven.

Sing "God So Loved."

Discussion starter video (5 minutes)

• "Unit 25 Session 2" discussion starter video

Leader • Let's answer our big picture question. ***Where did Jesus come from? God sent Jesus to earth from heaven.*** John the Baptist told his followers some reasons why Jesus is greater than John. How important is it that you are the best at something? Let's watch this video.

Show the "Unit 25 Session 2" video.

Leader • Have you ever wanted to be the best at something? It's OK to want to do well on a test or in a basketball game, but think about what John said. John said that Jesus must become greater and John must become less. John didn't want people to think he was so great that they didn't pay attention to Jesus.

What about you? Do you give Jesus the honor He deserves? Do you want to make Jesus famous or do you want to make yourself famous?

Sing (3 minutes)

• "The Only Name (Yours Will Be)" song

Leader • John told his followers that Jesus must become greater, and he (John) must become less. Why did John say that? John understood who Jesus is. Jesus comes from heaven and is more important than anyone else. John said that God the Father loves His Son, Jesus, and God gives Jesus power over everything.

Let's praise God for sending Jesus to earth as the

promised Messiah. Sing our theme song with me.
Lead boys and girls to sing "The Only Name (Yours Will Be)."

Prayer (2 minutes)

Leader • *Where did Jesus come from? God sent Jesus to earth from heaven.*

That's right! When Jesus taught, He often told people things about God's kingdom. He talked about what life is like when God is in charge. Even though some people did not believe the things Jesus said, Jesus was telling the truth. Jesus came from heaven, so He knew what He was talking about!

Let's pray, and then you can go to your small groups. God, thank You for sending Your Son, Jesus, to earth. We know that Jesus tells the truth about You and Your kingdom. You have given Him power over everything, and when we believe in Him, we will have eternal life. Thank You for the gift of salvation. Amen.

Dismiss to small groups

The Gospel: God's Plan for Me

Ask kids if they have ever heard the word *gospel*. Clarify that the word *gospel* means "good news." It is the message about Christ, the kingdom of God, and salvation. Use the following guide to share the gospel with kids.

God rules. Explain to kids that the Bible tells us God created everything, and He is in charge of everything. Invite a volunteer to read Genesis 1:1 from the Bible. Read Revelation 4:11 or Colossians 1:16-17 aloud and explain what these verses mean.

We sinned. Tell kids that since the time of Adam and Eve, everyone has chosen to disobey God. (Romans 3:23) The Bible calls this sin. Because God is holy, God cannot be around sin. Sin separates us from God and deserves God's punishment of death. (Romans 6:23)

God provided. Choose a child to read John 3:16 aloud. Say that God sent His Son, Jesus, the perfect solution to our sin problem, to rescue us from the punishment we deserve. It's something we, as sinners, could never earn on our own. Jesus alone saves us. Read and explain Ephesians 2:8-9.

Jesus gives. Share with kids that Jesus lived a perfect life, died on the cross for our sins, and rose again. Because Jesus gave up His life for us, we can be welcomed into God's family for eternity. This is the best gift ever! Read Romans 5:8; 2 Corinthians 5:21; or 1 Peter 3:18.

We respond. Tell kids that they can respond to Jesus. Read Romans 10:9-10,13. Review these aspects of our response: Believe in your heart that Jesus alone saves you through what He's already done on the cross. Repent, turning from self and sin to Jesus. Tell God and others that your faith is in Jesus.

Offer to talk with any child who is interested in responding to Jesus.

Small Group LEADER

Session Title: Jesus and John the Baptist
Bible Passage: John 3:22-36
Big Picture Question: Where did Jesus come from? God sent Jesus to earth from heaven.
Key Passage: John 3:16-17
Unit Christ Connection: Jesus was revealed as the fulfillment of Scripture, the promised Savior.

Key passage activity (5 minutes)

• Key Passage Poster

Form two or three groups of kids. Display the key passage poster. Lead kids in reading the key passage aloud together.

Point to a group. That group should begin reading the key passage. Point to a second group. The first group should stop reading, and the second group should pick up where the first group stopped. Continue pointing between the groups until kids recite the entire passage. As kids learn the verse, cover up parts of the key passage poster and challenge kids to recite the passage from memory.

Say • Well done. John the Baptist prepared the way for Jesus. Why did Jesus come to earth? Jesus came to earth to save people from their sins.

Bible story review & Bible skills (10 minutes)

• Bibles, 1 per kid
• Small Group Visual Pack

Provide a Bible for each kid and guide kids to find John 3:22-36 in the Bible. Review the timeline in the small group visual pack. Retell or review the Bible story in your own words or use the bolded text of the Bible story script.

Ask the following review questions. Encourage kids to find the verse in the Bible passage that reveals the answer. When a kid finds the answer, she should stand. Remind kids not to shout out the answer. If kids need help, provide the Scripture reference. Call on someone who is standing to say the answer. Then tell kids to sit to hear the next question.

1. What did Jesus do in the countryside? (*He spent time with His disciples, and people were baptized; John 3:22*)

2. Who had a question for John the Baptist? (*John's followers, John 3:25-26*)

3. What did John's followers tell John? (*Jesus was baptizing people, and people were following Him; John 3:26*)

4. John said he was not whom? (*the Messiah, John 3:28*)

5. To which person at a wedding did John compare Jesus? (*the groom, John 3:29*)

6. To which person at a wedding did John compare himself? (*the groom's friend, John 3:29*)

7. Who did John say must become greater? (*Jesus, John 3:30*)

8. Whose words does Jesus speak? (*God's words, John 3:34*)

9. What will those who believe in the Son have? (*eternal life, John 3:36*)

10. Who will not have eternal life? (*those who refuse to believe in the Son, John 3:36*)

Say • Great job, everyone! Now say the big picture question and answer with me. ***Where did Jesus come from? God sent Jesus to earth from heaven.***

If you choose to review with boys and girls how to become a Christian, explain that kids are welcome to speak with you or another teacher if they have questions.

- **God rules.** God created and is in charge of everything. (Gen. 1:1; Rev. 4:11; Col. 1:16-17)
- **We sinned.** Since Adam and Eve, everyone has

chosen to disobey God. (Rom. 3:23; 6:23)

- **God provided.** God sent His Son, Jesus, to rescue us from the punishment we deserve. (John 3:16; Eph. 2:8-9)
- **Jesus gives.** Jesus lived a perfect life, died on the cross for our sins, and rose again so we can be welcomed into God's family. (Rom. 5:8; 2 Cor. 5:21; 1 Pet. 3:18)
- **We respond.** Believe that Jesus alone saves you. Repent. Tell God that your faith is in Jesus. (Rom. 10:9-10,13)

Activity choice (10 minutes)

- large sheets of paper, 2
- marker
- tape

Option 1: Greater or less?

Make two posters labeled *Greater* and *Less*. Hang them on opposite sides of the room. Form two groups of kids—lions and sheep. Encourage kids to roar and baa.

Explain that you will announce an action. Kids should determine if their assigned animal would be greater than the other animal at completing the task and then move to the appropriate sign. For example, if the action is "Climb trees," then the lions should move to the *Greater* sign, and the sheep should move to the *Less* sign.

Announce several actions, giving kids time to move.

1. Run up to 50 miles per hour. (*Lions are greater.*)
2. Eat grass and clover. (*Sheep are greater.*)
3. Eat zebras, birds, or buffalo. (*Lions are greater.*)
4. Produce wool for making sweaters, blankets, and coats. (*Sheep are greater.*)
5. Hunt in grassy plains and open woodland. (*Lions are greater.*)

If time allows, choose a volunteer to call out more actions or assign other animals for kids to compare.

Say • Each of these animals was greater than the other at certain tasks. Who needed to become less in the Bible story? (*John the Baptist*) Who needed to become greater? (*Jesus*) When Jesus began His ministry on earth, John's mission was complete.

Option 2: Mission complete

• paper
• marker

List on a piece of paper 5 to 10 tasks kids can complete in the classroom. Make two copies of the task list. Task suggestions include the following:

1. Count how many steps it takes to walk from one side of the room to the other.
2. Tell your leader your favorite color.
3. Do 10 jumping jacks.
4. Sing the "Happy Birthday" song.
5. Recite the key passage, John 3:16-17.

Form two teams. Provide each team with a prepared task list. Signal teams to begin. Kids should work with their teams to complete the tasks. When a team finishes, its players should sit down and shout, "Mission complete!"

Say • Finishing something you worked hard at feels great. John the Baptist told people to get ready for Jesus. Now that Jesus was there, John's mission was complete. John joyfully stepped aside as Jesus began His earthly ministry.

Journal and prayer (5 minutes)

• pencils
• journals
• Bibles
• Journal Page, 1 per kid (enhanced CD)
• "Are You the Messiah?" activity page, 1 per kid

Say • Draw or write in your journal about a talent or ability you have that you could use to tell people about Jesus.

After a few minutes, invite kids to share prayer requests. Close the group in prayer. As time allows, lead kids to complete the activity page "Are You the Messiah?" by writing the descriptions in the correct circles.

Leader BIBLE STUDY

At the time Jesus was on earth, the social food chain went like this: Jews didn't talk to Samaritans. The strife between the two groups stretched back hundreds of years to the Babylonian exile.

When the Babylonians attacked Judah, they moved a large group of God's people away from their homes. But some of the people—the poorest, sickest, least able to work—were left behind in the region that became known as Samaria. The exile lasted 70 years. During that time, those left in Samaria began to mingle with their neighbors to the north. They intermarried and practiced foreign customs. While the Samaritans still believed in God, the Samaritans adapted their beliefs and set up their own place of worship on Mount Gerizim. (See 2 Kings 17:29-41; Ezra 9:1-2.)

The Jews who returned home from Babylon to rebuild God's temple in Jerusalem rejected this new way of life. They were dedicated to obeying and worshiping God, and they didn't agree with the Samaritans' practices. The Samaritans opposed the Jews' efforts to reestablish their nation. In time, the Jews' hate for the Samaritans grew—so much so, that a Jew traveling from Judea to Galilee would take a longer route to travel around Samaria rather than through it.

Jesus broke down barriers when He traveled to Galilee by way of Samaria. Even more surprising, Jesus stopped at a well around noon and asked a Samaritan woman for a drink. Jewish men did not speak to women in public.

But Jesus was kind to her, and He offered a gift—living water. The woman didn't understand, but Jesus revealed His knowledge of her past. He even gave her a glimpse of the future. The Samaritan woman expected a Messiah to come and fix everything. Jesus said, "I am He."

The living water Jesus offers is the Holy Spirit. (See John 7:37-39.) It is a gift that He is eager to give us when we ask Him. Those who receive His grace will never be thirsty again.

Older Kids BIBLE STUDY OVERVIEW

Session Title: Jesus Met a Samaritan Woman
Bible Passage: John 4:1-26
Big Picture Question: What does Jesus offer? Jesus offers eternal life.
Key Passage: John 3:16-17
Unit Christ Connection: Jesus was revealed as the fulfillment of
   Scripture, the promised Savior.

Small Group Opening

Large Group Leader

Small Group Leader

The BIBLE STORY

Jesus Met a Samaritan Woman
John 4:1-26

Jesus had been making disciples in Judea, and His disciples baptized people. Now Jesus had more followers than John the Baptist. **The time came for Jesus to leave Judea.**

Jesus began traveling back to Galilee. Usually, people who were Jews took the long route between Judea and Galilee because in between these two places was Samaria. Jews did not like people from Samaria. The two groups of people had not gotten along for many, many years. So Jews avoided Samaritans whenever they could.

But Jesus was not like all the other Jews. He traveled straight through Samaria. While He was there, He stopped in a town at the well. The sun was high overhead. Jesus' disciples went into town to buy food.

While Jesus was at the well, a Samaritan woman came to get water from the well.

"Give Me a drink," Jesus said to the woman.

The woman was surprised. **"You're a Jew," she said. "Why are you talking to me? I'm a Samaritan."**

Jesus said, "I asked you for a drink. You don't know who I am. If you did, you would have asked Me for a drink, and I would give you living water."

The woman was confused. Jesus didn't look like He had any water; He didn't even have a bucket to get water out of the well.

"Sir," the woman said, "This well is deep, and you don't have a bucket. Where do You get this 'living water'?"

Jesus said, "Anyone who drinks this well water will be thirsty again, but whoever drinks from the water I give will never, ever get thirsty again! In fact, the water I give will become a well inside you, and you will have eternal life." Now Jesus was talking about the Holy Spirit, but the woman did not understand.

"Sir," she said, "give me this water. If I'm not thirsty, I won't have to keep coming to this well to get water."

"Go get your husband," Jesus said.

"I don't have a husband," the woman replied.

Jesus knew she was telling the truth. "That's right," He said. "You don't have a husband now, but you've had five husbands."

Jesus was right. "I see you are a prophet," the woman said. Maybe this prophet could explain something to her that she didn't understand. She said, "The Samaritans worship here on a mountain, but the Jews say we need to worship at the temple in Jerusalem."

Jesus said, "Soon you will not need to be in either of those places to worship God in spirit and in truth."

The woman said, "I know the Messiah is coming. When He comes, He will explain everything to us."

Then Jesus said, "He is talking to you now. I am the Messiah."

Christ Connection: Jesus offered the woman something no one else could give her—living water. Jesus wasn't talking about water that she could physically drink; Jesus was talking about the Holy Spirit who would satisfy her spiritual thirst. Jesus gives the Holy Spirit to those who come to Him by faith.

Small Group OPENING

Session Title: Jesus Met a Samaritan Woman
Bible Passage: John 4:1-26
Big Picture Question: What does Jesus offer? Jesus offers eternal life.
Key Passage: John 3:16-17
Unit Christ Connection: Jesus was revealed as the fulfillment of Scripture, the promised Savior.

Welcome time

Greet each kid as he or she arrives. Use this time to collect the offering, fill out attendance sheets, and help new kids connect to your group. Invite kids to share their favorite things to drink when they are thirsty.

Activity page (5 minutes)

• "Well, Well" activity page, 1 per kid
• pencils

Guide kids to complete the activity page "Well, Well." Help kids follow the instructions. They should begin with their pencil on the start space and then skip to every other stone, writing down the letters as they move around the well. Kids will circle the well twice to discover something Jesus said to a Samaritan woman in today's Bible story.

Say • Did you solve the puzzle? What did Jesus say to the woman at the well? (*"Give Me a drink," John 4:7*) We'll hear about Jesus and the Samaritan woman in today's Bible story.

Session starter (10 minutes)

Option 1: Picture words

• large sheets of paper
• marker

Invite kids to play a guessing game. Choose a volunteer to be the artist. Whisper to the artist one of the following picture words: *bucket, well, water, drink, woman,* or *husband*. Kids should try to guess what the artist is drawing. The artist may not speak or write any letters or words on the paper. When a kid guesses what the artist has drawn, choose another volunteer to be the artist. Play several rounds.

Say • Does anyone know what all these pictures have in common? They are all pictures of things in the Bible story we are going to hear today.

Option 2: Bucket-ball relay

- buckets, 2
- foam balls or paper wads, 8
- masking tape or painter's tape

Form two teams of kids. Direct each team to stand in a single-file line. Position four foam balls and one bucket at the front of each line. At the end of each line, mark a square on the floor with tape.

Explain the rules of the game. When you say go, the first kid in line will pick up a bucket and put one ball inside. He will then pass the bucket to the second player. Players must pass the bucket down the line until it reaches the last player. The last player will put the ball in the square and then pass the bucket back up the line. Each player must take a turn passing the bucket. When the bucket returns to the first player, he will put another ball in the bucket and pass it back down the line.

Continue play until teams have moved all the balls into the square at the end of the line. When a team finishes, players should sit down.

Say • Good work, everyone! Today we are going to hear a story from the Bible about a woman Jesus met at a well. The woman went to the well every day to collect water with a bucket.

Transition to large group

Large Group LEADER

Session Title: Jesus Met a Samaritan Woman
Bible Passage: John 4:1-26
Big Picture Question: What does Jesus offer? Jesus offers eternal life.
Key Passage: John 3:16-17
Unit Christ Connection: Jesus was revealed as the fulfillment of
Scripture, the promised Savior.

Countdown

• countdown video

Show the countdown video as your kids arrive, and set it to
end as large group time begins.

Introduce the session (2 minutes)

• leader attire
• map

*[Large Group Leader enters wearing a name tag, a hat
or visor, and a button that says "Ask Me!" Leader is also
carrying a map.]*

Leader •Welcome, everyone! In case you forgot, my name
is [*your name*]. We have been learning a lot about Jesus'
early ministry. Did you know that Jesus spent three years
teaching people before He died on the cross? During that
time, Jesus met a lot of people. I don't know about you,
but I love meeting new people. I think Jesus did too. Let's
get started.

Timeline map (2 minutes)

• Timeline Map

Use the timeline map to point out and review the previous
Bible stories, "Jesus Met Nicodemus" and "Jesus and John
the Baptist."

Leader •Look at our timeline map. Do you remember
who came to visit Jesus at night? (*Nicodemus*) Jesus told
Nicodemus about God's great plan to save people from

sin. Jesus also told him that to enter God's kingdom, a person needs to be born again. ***Why do we need to be born again? Because of sin we are spiritually dead, but Jesus came to give us new life.***

Then we learned about Jesus and John the Baptist. John told people to get ready for Jesus, the promised Messiah. Now that Jesus was there, John's mission was complete. John joyfully stepped aside as Jesus began His ministry. Today, we're going to hear about someone else Jesus met.

Big picture question (1 minute)

Leader • With a new Bible story today, we have a new big picture question. Are you ready for it? OK. Our big picture question is, ***What does Jesus offer?*** Listen carefully to the Bible story and see if you can figure out the answer.

Tell the Bible story (10 minutes)

- "Jesus Met a Samaritan Woman" video
- Bibles, 1 per kid
- Bible Story Picture Slide or Poster
- Big Picture Question Slide or Poster
- "Map Through Samaria" (enhanced CD)

Open your Bible to John 4:1-26 and tell the Bible story in your own words or show the Bible story video "Jesus Met a Samaritan Woman." As you review the Bible story, display the map to point out the route Jesus took through Samaria.

Leader • Jesus had been in Judea. His disciples baptized people, and people began following Jesus. When it was time for Jesus to leave Judea and go back to Galilee, He and His disciples started traveling north.

Between the land of Judea and the land of Galilee was the land of Samaria. Most Jews did not travel through Samaria. They went around the land instead. Do you remember why? (*Jews and Samaritans did not get along.*)

But Jesus was not like other Jews. He loves everyone, and He traveled right through the land of Samaria. Jesus and the disciples came to a town. The disciples went to get something to eat, and Jesus sat down at the well. He was tired from traveling. A Samaritan woman came to the well to get water. What did Jesus say to the woman? (*"Give Me a drink."*)

The woman was surprised that Jesus, a Jew, was talking to her, a Samaritan. Jesus offered the woman living water. He said that this water was a gift from God. Jesus wasn't talking about actual water like the water that came from the well. He was offering the woman something else.

What does Jesus offer? Jesus offers eternal life. That's our big picture question and answer. Let's say it together. **What does Jesus offer? Jesus offers eternal life.**

Jesus was talking about the Holy Spirit. Eternal life is a free gift. Jesus gives the Holy Spirit to those who come to Him by faith. When we trust in Jesus as Lord and Savior, He saves us from our sins.

The Gospel: God's Plan for Me (optional)

• Bible

Using Scripture and the guide provided, explain to boys and girls how to become a Christian. Tell kids how they can respond, and provide counselors to speak with each kid individually. Encourage boys and girls to ask their parents, small group leaders, or other adults any questions they may have about becoming a Christian.

Key passage (5 minutes)

• Key Passage Slide or Poster
• "God So Loved" song

Leader • Jesus offered the woman at the well living water. God showed His love for us by sending Jesus into the world. Jesus came to die the death we deserve for our sin. Let's review our key passage.

Instruct kids to find John 3:16-17 in their Bibles. Help them as needed. Choose a few volunteers to take turns reading the key passage aloud.

Leader •Can anyone tell me who said these words? (*Jesus said them to Nicodemus.*) Jesus told Nicodemus about God's great plan for the world. He told Nicodemus how a person can have eternal life.

Do people have eternal life by doing good things? (*No.*)

How do people have eternal life? (*by believing in Jesus*) Sing "God So Loved."

Discussion starter video (5 minutes)

• "Unit 25 Session 3" discussion starter video

Leader •Jesus told the Samaritan woman that He could give her living water. He said that anyone who drinks this living water would never be thirsty again.

Do you think the Samaritan woman thought that sounded too good to be true? Have you ever heard about something that sounded too good to be true? Think about that as we watch this video.

Show the "Unit 25 Session 3" video. Then invite kids to describe things they've heard of that sounded too good to be true. Were they?

Leader •Jesus offers living water. It sounds too good to be true, but it *is* true! The living water Jesus is talking about is the Holy Spirit. Jesus gives the Holy Spirit to those who trust in Him. He saves us from our sins and gives us eternal life.

Sing (3 minutes)

• "The Only Name (Yours Will Be)" song

Leader •The Bible says that the only way to get to God is by trusting in Jesus. Jesus offers us salvation as a free gift. We can't do anything to earn it.

Open your Bible to John 14:6 and read the verse aloud. Then invite kids to sing together the theme song, "The Only Name (Yours Will Be)."

Prayer (2 minutes)

Leader • *What does Jesus offer? Jesus offers eternal life.*
Deep down, everyone has a spiritual thirst—a longing
that only God can satisfy. Some people try to satisfy this
thirst with other things, like money or relationships or
popularity, but they are still thirsty for something more.

Jesus told the Samaritan woman that He could give her
living water so she would never be thirsty again. Jesus
offers us living water too. He offers us eternal life. Let's
pray.

God, thank You for sending Jesus to die on the cross
for our sins to satisfy our greatest thirst—our thirst for
You. Please forgive us for trying to find happiness in other
things. Only You can satisfy us. We love You, and we
want to know You more. Amen.

Dismiss to small groups

The Gospel: God's Plan for Me

Ask kids if they have ever heard the word *gospel*. Clarify that the word *gospel* means "good news." It is the message about Christ, the kingdom of God, and salvation. Use the following guide to share the gospel with kids.

God rules. Explain to kids that the Bible tells us God created everything, and He is in charge of everything. Invite a volunteer to read Genesis 1:1 from the Bible. Read Revelation 4:11 or Colossians 1:16-17 aloud and explain what these verses mean.

We sinned. Tell kids that since the time of Adam and Eve, everyone has chosen to disobey God. (Romans 3:23) The Bible calls this sin. Because God is holy, God cannot be around sin. Sin separates us from God and deserves God's punishment of death. (Romans 6:23)

God provided. Choose a child to read John 3:16 aloud. Say that God sent His Son, Jesus, the perfect solution to our sin problem, to rescue us from the punishment we deserve. It's something we, as sinners, could never earn on our own. Jesus alone saves us. Read and explain Ephesians 2:8-9.

Jesus gives. Share with kids that Jesus lived a perfect life, died on the cross for our sins, and rose again. Because Jesus gave up His life for us, we can be welcomed into God's family for eternity. This is the best gift ever! Read Romans 5:8; 2 Corinthians 5:21; or 1 Peter 3:18.

We respond. Tell kids that they can respond to Jesus. Read Romans 10:9-10,13. Review these aspects of our response: Believe in your heart that Jesus alone saves you through what He's already done on the cross. Repent, turning from self and sin to Jesus. Tell God and others that your faith is in Jesus.

Offer to talk with any child who is interested in responding to Jesus.

Small Group LEADER

Session Title: Jesus Met a Samaritan Woman
Bible Passage: John 4:1-26
Big Picture Question: What does Jesus offer? Jesus offers eternal life.
Key Passage: John 3:16-17
Unit Christ Connection: Jesus was revealed as the fulfillment of
Scripture, the promised Savior.

Key passage activity (5 minutes)

- Key Passage Poster
- index cards,
  1 per kid
- tape
- marker

Write words or phrases of the key passage on separate index
cards. Make one card per kid. Distribute the cards and assist
kids in taping the cards to their shirts.

When you say go, kids should work together to arrange
themselves in the correct order of the key passage. When
kids finish, invite them to say the key passage aloud. Each
kid should say the word written on his card. Allow kids to
make any necessary corrections if anyone is out of order.

Say • *What does Jesus offer? Jesus offers eternal life.* The
Bible says that people who believe in Jesus will have
eternal life. Does having eternal life mean we will
never die a physical death? (*No.*) Having eternal life
means that even death won't keep us from life with
God forever.

Bible story review & Bible skills (10 minutes)

- Bibles, 1 per kid
- Small Group Visual
  Pack

Guide kids to find John 4 in the Bible. Encourage kids to
use the table of contents if they need help.

Say • Which division of the Bible is the Book of John in?
(*Gospels*) What do the Gospels tell us about? (*Jesus'
life, death, and resurrection*) What books come
before and after the Book of John? (*the Book of Luke*

and the Book of Acts)

Review the timeline in the small group visual pack. Invite a volunteer to retell or review the Bible story in his own words. Ask kids to supply any details the volunteer may have left out. Then encourage kids to use the Bible to answer to following review questions:

1. Where did Jesus stop during His journey to Galilee? (*at a well in Samaria, John 4:3-6*)
2. Whom did Jesus meet at the well? (*a Samaritan woman, John 4:7*)
3. What did Jesus say to the woman? (*"Give Me a drink," John 4:7*)
4. Why was the woman surprised that Jesus was talking to her? (*Jesus was a Jew, and she was a Samaritan; John 4:9*)
5. What kind of water did Jesus say He could give the woman? (*living water, John 4:10*)
6. Whom did Jesus tell the woman to bring to the well? (*her husband, John 4:16*)
7. Who did the woman know was coming? (*the Messiah, John 4:25*)
8. Who did Jesus tell the woman He is? (*the Messiah, John 4:26*)
9. ***What does Jesus offer? Jesus offers eternal life.***

If you choose to review with boys and girls how to become a Christian, explain that kids are welcome to speak with you or another teacher if they have questions.

- **God rules.** God created and is in charge of everything. (Gen. 1:1; Rev. 4:11; Col. 1:16-17)
- **We sinned.** Since Adam and Eve, everyone has chosen to disobey God. (Rom. 3:23; 6:23)
- **God provided.** God sent His Son, Jesus, to rescue us from the punishment we deserve. (John 3:16; Eph. 2:8-9)

- **Jesus gives.** Jesus lived a perfect life, died on the cross for our sins, and rose again so we can be welcomed into God's family. (Rom. 5:8; 2 Cor. 5:21; 1 Pet. 3:18)
- **We respond.** Believe that Jesus alone saves you. Repent. Tell God that your faith is in Jesus. (Rom. 10:9-10,13)

Activity choice (10 minutes)

- index cards
- marker

Option 1: A good guess

Write the following words on separate index cards: *awake, blanket, flag, frown, hippopotamus, island, penguin, rain, smell, straw, watermelon.* If needed, make extra word cards.

Choose a volunteer to be the first player. Give her a word card. The player should look at the word and then set the card aside facedown. The player should use words or gestures to lead the rest of the kids to guess what word was written on the card. She may not say the actual word. If a player has the word *penguin*, she could waddle with her hands to the side and say, "an animal that is black and white and lives in cold places like Antarctica."

When a kid guesses the correct word, invite him to lead the next round. Give several kids a chance to describe or act out the words on the cards.

Say • You did a good job guessing what was written on the cards. In the Bible story, Jesus knew everything about the Samaritan woman. He knew about her husbands, and He knew her greatest need—to be saved from sin. Jesus offered the woman a gift.

- ***What does Jesus offer? Jesus offers eternal life.*** Jesus knows us and our needs. He does not have to guess what is going on in our lives. We can trust in Him for salvation and eternal life.

Option 2: Bottled water labels

• "Bottled Water Labels" (enhanced CD)
• bottles of water
• markers
• tape

Print and cut apart the bottled water labels in the translation you use. Prepare enough labels for each kid to have one or two.

Provide kids with markers and labels. Invite them to color and decorate the labels. Then demonstrate how to tape a label around a bottle of water. Encourage kids to share unopened bottles of water with friends or family members, or arrange to provide bottled water to local group in need.

As kids work, review the Bible story. Help kids understand that the living water Jesus offered the woman wasn't like the water the woman drew from the well. When Jesus talked about living water, He was talking about the Holy Spirit. The Holy Spirit satisfies people's spiritual thirst for a relationship with God. Jesus gives the Holy Spirit to those who come to Him by faith.

Say • *What does Jesus offer? Jesus offers eternal life.*

• Jesus said that whoever drinks from the water that He gives will never get thirsty again—ever!

Journal and prayer (5 minutes)

• pencils
• journals
• Bibles
• Journal Page, 1 per kid (enhanced CD)
• "Endless H$_2$O" activity page, 1 per kid

Encourage kids to list in their journals the names of classmates or neighbors who might sometimes feel lonely. Invite kids to spend a few minutes praying for these people.

Say • Jesus talked to the Samaritan woman even though Jews didn't usually talk to Samaritans. Jesus offers salvation to everyone.

Invite kids to share prayer requests. Close the group in prayer, or allow a couple volunteers to close the group in prayer. As time allows, lead kids to complete the activity page "Endless H$_2$O."

Leader BIBLE STUDY

Jesus was about thirty years old when He began His ministry. After John baptized Jesus in the Jordan River, Jesus was tempted in the desert. Jesus traveled to Jerusalem for the Passover. Then, He headed north to Galilee. He went through the region of Samaria, stopping at Jacob's well to talk to a Samaritan woman.

Jesus began teaching in the synagogues. He went to the town of Nazareth. Nazareth was a small village in the hills between the Sea of Galilee and the Mediterranean Sea. This was the place Jesus grew up.

On the Sabbath day, Jesus went into the synagogue. He read aloud the words of the prophet Isaiah. (See Isa. 61:1-2.) Jesus sat down. Everyone's eyes were on Him as He explained, "Today as you listen, this Scripture has been fulfilled." What was Jesus saying? Jesus was saying, *It's Me*. The words Jesus read were coming true. Some of the people might have remembered Jesus from His youth. They asked, "Isn't this Joseph's son?"

Jesus knew their thoughts; Jesus had performed miracles in Capernaum, and the people wanted Jesus to do miracles in His hometown too. Jesus reminded them of two Old Testament accounts. Many widows lived in Israel when the prophet Elijah was there, but God sent Elijah to help a widow in another country. And Elisha likely encountered Israelites who had leprosy, but he healed Naaman the Syrian.

Jesus wanted the people to understand that His miracles were an act of grace—a gift. No one deserves God's grace, so God may show grace to whomever He pleases. The people were angry. They drove Jesus away, intending to kill Him, but Jesus escaped through the crowd.

Jesus came to give sight to the blind and to set the captives free. He came preaching good news. Finally, the Messiah had come! Jesus is God's plan to save sinners.

Older Kids BIBLE STUDY OVERVIEW

Session Title: Rejection at Nazareth
Bible Passage: Luke 4:16-30
Big Picture Question: What is the good news about Jesus? Jesus died for our sins.
Key Passage: John 3:16-17
Unit Christ Connection: Jesus was revealed as the fulfillment of Scripture, the promised Savior.

Small Group Opening

Large Group Leader

Small Group Leader

The BIBLE STORY

Rejection at Nazareth
Luke 4:16-30

Jesus went to Nazareth. Nazareth was Jesus' hometown; He grew up there. **On the Sabbath day, Jesus went to the synagogue** like He usually did.

The Sabbath day was a holy day of rest. On that day, the Jews gathered in the synagogue to worship God. The synagogue was a special building where Jews met together to pray, worship, and learn about the Scriptures.

Jesus stood up to read Scripture. He unrolled the scroll of the prophet Isaiah. Then He read from the place where these words were written: **"The Spirit of the Lord is on Me. He has chosen Me to tell good news to the poor. He has sent Me to tell the captives that they are free, to tell the blind that they can see, to free people who have been treated badly, and to announce that the Lord's favor is on us."** Then **Jesus rolled up the scroll. He gave it back to the attendant and sat down.**

Everyone who was in the synagogue stared at Jesus. They watched Him closely, and **Jesus said, "Today as you listened to Me reading these words, they came true."**

The people said good things about Jesus, and they were amazed to hear Him say such wonderful things. **But some of the people** in Nazareth had known Jesus from His youth. They **wondered how this was possible. "Isn't this Joseph's son?" they asked.**

Jesus was Joseph's son, but He was far from ordinary. **Even though Jesus' earthly father was Joseph, His true Father is God.**

Then Jesus said to them, "You will probably say this old proverb: 'Doctor, heal yourself.' **You've heard about the miracles I performed in Capernaum, and you want me to do them here in My hometown too."**

Jesus also said, "No prophet is accepted in his hometown." **Jesus reminded the people of the prophets Elijah and Elisha.** When **there was a terrible famine in Israel**, and no rain fell there for three and a half years, plenty of widows in the country needed help.

But Elijah did not help the widows in Israel. Instead, **God sent Elijah**

to help a widow in another land.

And **when Elisha was a prophet,** many people in Israel had leprosy. They wanted to be healed, but Elisha did not heal them. Instead, **he healed a man named Naaman** (NAY muhn), and **Naaman was from Syria**—a country that did not get along with God's people.

The people listening to Jesus in the synagogue were angry. They got up and forced Jesus out of town. They wanted to throw Him off a cliff, but Jesus walked right through the crowd and went on His way.

Christ Connection: Hundreds of years before Jesus was born, the prophet Isaiah wrote about God's plan to send a Messiah. He would bring good news and redeem people who were broken and hurting. Jesus read Isaiah's words and told everyone who was listening that He is the promised Messiah.

Small Group OPENING

Session Title: Rejection at Nazareth
Bible Passage: Luke 4:16-30
Big Picture Question: What is the good news about Jesus? Jesus died for our sins.
Key Passage: John 3:16-17
Unit Christ Connection: Jesus was revealed as the fulfillment of Scripture, the promised Savior.

Welcome time

Greet each kid as he or she arrives. Use this time to collect the offering, fill out attendance sheets, and help new kids connect to your group. Prompt kids to share some facts about their hometowns. If a kid's family has moved away from his hometown, ask if he has ever gone back to visit.

Activity page (5 minutes)

• "Good News Word Ladder" activity page, 1 per kid
• pencils

Allow kids to work in pairs or small groups to complete the "Good News Word Ladder" activity page. Kids will begin at the bottom. To move up the ladder, read each clue and follow the steps to create new words. Assist kids if needed. (*good, mood, moo, boo, boot, foot, dot, net, new, news*)

Say • How do you react when you hear good news? Today we are going to hear a story from the Bible about the good news Jesus brought to people on earth.

Session starter (10 minutes)

Option 1: Good words

Play a synonym game. Invite the kids to work together or form groups for a competition. Provide each group with a marker and piece of paper. One kid in each group will be

• large pieces of paper
• marker

the writer. The writer should list the letters *A* through *T* on the paper. At your signal, teams will list for each letter a word that relates to *good*. If teams struggle to think of synonyms, invite them to list people, places, or things that they think of when they hear the word *good*.

Give kids several minutes to work. Then call on kids to share their lists. Invite the class to fill in any blanks on their lists. Suggest words as needed: *awesome*, *cool*, *excellent*, *favorable*, *great*, *marvelous*, *positive*, *super*, and so forth.

Say • The Bible says that God is good. (Ps. 100:5) In our Bible story today, Jesus brought some good news to the people in His hometown, but not everyone thought the news was good.

Option 2: Newspaper sculptures

• newspapers
• masking tape
• wet wipes
  (optional)

Invite kids to work in small groups to create newspaper sculptures. Provide each group with masking tape and several pages of newspaper. Demonstrate how to crumple and twist the newspaper to form different shapes. Explain that kids can use the masking tape to hold their newspaper pieces together. Give kids several minutes to sculpt whatever they desire.

Lead each group to share its creation with the rest of the kids and to describe any difficulties they encountered while sculpting. Provide wet wipes to clean up any ink from the newspaper that may have dirtied kids' hands.

Say • Many people read newspapers to find out the news. Newspapers are filled with good news and bad news. Today's Bible story is about some good news Jesus shared with the people in His hometown.

Transition to large group

Large Group LEADER

Session Title: Rejection at Nazareth
Bible Passage: Luke 4:16-30
Big Picture Question: What is the good news about Jesus? Jesus died for our sins.
Key Passage: John 3:16-17
Unit Christ Connection: Jesus was revealed as the fulfillment of Scripture, the promised Savior.

Countdown

• countdown video

Show the countdown video as your kids arrive, and set it to end as large group time begins.

Introduce the session (2 minutes)

• leader attire
• map

[Large Group Leader enters wearing a name tag, a hat or visor, and a button that says "Ask Me!" Leader is also carrying a map.]

Leader • Today will be our last visit to the theme park. I've had so much fun with you. You have done a great job discovering the answers to our big picture questions. Are you ready to get started? First, let's take a look back at where we've been so far.

Timeline map (2 minutes)

• Timeline Map

Use the timeline map to point out and review the previous Bible stories: "Jesus Met Nicodemus," "Jesus and John the Baptist," and "Jesus Met a Samaritan Woman."

Leader • Do you remember these Bible stories? Nicodemus came to Jesus at night, and Jesus told him about God's great plan to save people from sin. He told Nicodemus that a person needs to be born again to go to heaven.

Why do we need to be born again? Because of sin we are spiritually dead, but Jesus came to give us new life.

Do you remember what John the Baptist's job was? That's right. He told people to get ready for Jesus. Now that Jesus was there, John's mission was complete. Then from the story "Jesus Met a Samaritan Woman," we learned that Jesus offers something to us. *What does Jesus offer? Jesus offers eternal life.*

Jesus had good news for the world, but in the Bible story we are going to hear today, some people did not want to hear what Jesus had to say.

Big picture question (1 minute)

Leader • That leads me to our big picture question: *What is the good news about Jesus?* The good news that Jesus brought to people made some of the people angry. Listen to the Bible story to find out what happened.

Tell the Bible story (10 minutes)

• "Rejection at Nazareth" video
• Bibles
• Bible Story Picture Slide or Poster
• Big Picture Question Slide or Poster

Open your Bible to Luke 4:16-30 and tell the Bible story in your own words or show the Bible story video "Rejection at Nazareth."

Leader • Nazareth was Jesus' hometown. Remember, Jesus was born in Bethlehem when Mary and Joseph traveled there to be counted for a census. When Jesus was still young, Mary and Joseph took Him to Nazareth, and Jesus grew up there. (Matt. 2:19-22)

Jesus went into the synagogue in Nazareth to teach on the Sabbath. He read from the scroll of the prophet Isaiah. What were the words that Jesus read from the scroll? Call on a volunteer to read aloud Luke 4:18-19 from the Bible.

Leader • When Jesus read these words, He said, "Today

as you listen, this Scripture has been fulfilled." What did Jesus mean? Jesus was saying that those words Isaiah wrote were talking about Him! God chose Jesus to preach good news to the poor, to tell the captives that they are free, and to tell the blind that they can see. God promised throughout the Old Testament that a Messiah would come to rescue God's people. Jesus is the promised Messiah!

Many of the people in the crowd said good things about Jesus, but some of the people wondered if Jesus was telling the truth. After all, they had seen Jesus grow up in Nazareth. Could He really be the Messiah?

Then Jesus talked about the miracles some of the prophets, like Elijah and Elisha, did in the Old Testament. God had done good things for many people, not just the Jewish people. This made some of the people in the synagogue angry, and they forced Jesus out of town. They wanted to throw Jesus off a cliff, but Jesus walked away.

The prophet Isaiah wrote that the Messiah would tell good news to the poor. Jesus came to earth to save people from their sins. Jesus never sinned, but He took the punishment we deserve when He died on the cross. Everyone who trusts in Him is declared righteous, and they will have eternal life.

What is the good news about Jesus? Jesus died for our sins. That's our big picture question and answer. Say it with me. *What is the good news about Jesus? Jesus died for our sins.*

The Gospel: God's Plan for Me (optional)

• Bible

Using Scripture and the guide provided, explain to boys and girls how to become a Christian. Tell kids how they can respond, and provide counselors to speak with each kid individually. Guide counselors to use open-ended questions to allow kids to determine the direction of the conversation. Encourage boys and girls to ask their parents, small group leaders, or other adults any questions they may have about becoming a Christian.

Key passage (5 minutes)

• Key Passage Slide or Poster
• "God So Loved" song

Leader • Some of the people who heard Jesus teach did not understand why He had come. They did not know that Jesus was part of God's great plan to save people from their sins. In our key passage, Jesus told why He had come to earth. Let's practice it together.

Guide kids to find John 3:16-17 in their Bibles. Designate John 3:16 to half of the group and John 3:17 to the other half. Call on each group to recite its assigned verse in turn. Then swap assignments and call for kids to recite the passage again.

Leader • Jesus said that God did not send Him into the world to condemn the world. The word *condemn* means "to declare guilty." The Bible says everyone has sinned, and we deserve to be punished for our sin. Jesus would be right to declare us guilty, but He came to take our punishment for us. That's good news!

Sing "God So Loved."

Discussion starter video (5 minutes)

• "Unit 25 Session 4" discussion starter video

Leader • The people in Jesus' hometown rejected Him. These were the people who had probably known Him the longest. They saw Him grow up from a young boy to a man. Being rejected doesn't feel good. Watch this.

Show the "Unit 25 Session 4" video.

Leader • How do you feel when you are left out or rejected?

Sing (3 minutes)

• "The Only Name (Yours Will Be)" song

Leader • Jesus was rejected in His hometown. Other people might sometimes reject us because of how we look, what we like, or because we love Jesus. But Jesus will never reject us when we turn to Him. [*See John 6:37.*] We can trust Him for our salvation. Let's praise Him together. Lead boys and girls to sing "The Only Name (Yours Will Be)."

Prayer (2 minutes)

Leader • *What is the good news about Jesus? Jesus died for our sins.* This is the gospel. Our sin separates us from God, and we could never be good enough to get to God on our own. But Jesus died on the cross, and we can trust in Him as Lord and Savior. Jesus came to rescue us from sin so we can be with God forever.

Let's pray before you go to your small groups. Lord God, You are good. We do not deserve Your grace, but You sent Jesus because You love us. Thank You for the gift of salvation. Amen.

Dismiss to small groups

The Gospel: God's Plan for Me

Ask kids if they have ever heard the word *gospel*. Clarify that the word *gospel* means "good news." It is the message about Christ, the kingdom of God, and salvation. Use the following guide to share the gospel with kids.

God rules. Explain to kids that the Bible tells us God created everything, and He is in charge of everything. Invite a volunteer to read Genesis 1:1 from the Bible. Read Revelation 4:11 or Colossians 1:16-17 aloud and explain what these verses mean.

We sinned. Tell kids that since the time of Adam and Eve, everyone has chosen to disobey God. (Romans 3:23) The Bible calls this sin. Because God is holy, God cannot be around sin. Sin separates us from God and deserves God's punishment of death. (Romans 6:23)

God provided. Choose a child to read John 3:16 aloud. Say that God sent His Son, Jesus, the perfect solution to our sin problem, to rescue us from the punishment we deserve. It's something we, as sinners, could never earn on our own. Jesus alone saves us. Read and explain Ephesians 2:8-9.

Jesus gives. Share with kids that Jesus lived a perfect life, died on the cross for our sins, and rose again. Because Jesus gave up His life for us, we can be welcomed into God's family for eternity. This is the best gift ever! Read Romans 5:8; 2 Corinthians 5:21; or 1 Peter 3:18.

We respond. Tell kids that they can respond to Jesus. Read Romans 10:9-10,13. Review these aspects of our response: Believe in your heart that Jesus alone saves you through what He's already done on the cross. Repent, turning from self and sin to Jesus. Tell God and others that your faith is in Jesus.

Offer to talk with any child who is interested in responding to Jesus.

Small Group LEADER

Session Title: Rejection at Nazareth
Bible Passage: Luke 4:16-30
Big Picture Question: What is the good news about Jesus? Jesus died for our sins.
Key Passage: John 3:16-17
Unit Christ Connection: Jesus was revealed as the fulfillment of Scripture, the promised Savior.

Key passage activity (5 minutes)

• Key Passage Poster
• index cards
• marker

Write words or phrases of the key passage on separate index cards. Make two sets. Scatter each set on the floor. Form two groups of kids and guide them to line up several feet from their group's set of key passage cards.

When you say go, the first kid in each group should run to the cards and pick up the first word or phrase of the key passage. When she returns to her group, the next player will go pick up the second card. Continue until kids pick up the entire key passage in order. Then read the passage aloud.

Say • Our key passage tells us the gospel. The word *gospel* means "good news." *What is the good news about Jesus? Jesus died for our sins.*

Bible story review & Bible skills (10 minutes)

• Bibles, 1 per kid
• Small Group Visual Pack

Option: Retell or review the Bible story using the bolded text of the Bible story script.

Say • Open your Bibles to the Book of Luke. Can anyone tell me what book comes before Luke? (*Mark*) What book comes after Luke? (*John*) Great job. Remember, the four Gospels—Matthew, Mark, Luke, and John—all tell us about Jesus' life, death, and resurrection.

Review the timeline in the small group visual pack.

Form three groups of kids. Assign each group a different

passage: Luke 4:16-19; Luke 4:20-24; and Luke 4:25-30. Ask each group three of the following review questions corresponding to its passage. Kids should use their Bibles to find the answers. When kids answer, prompt them to tell you which verse or verses they read to find the answer.

1. In what town did Jesus grow up? (*Nazareth, Luke 4:16*)
2. Where did Jesus go on the Sabbath day? (*to the synagogue, Luke 4:16*)
3. From which part of Scripture did Jesus read? (*Isaiah, Luke 4:17*)
4. What did Jesus say after He read the Scripture? (*"Today as you listen, this Scripture has been fulfilled"; Luke 4:21*)
5. The people knew Jesus was whose son? (*Joseph's, Luke 4:22*)
6. Where did Jesus say no prophet is accepted? (*in his hometown, Luke 4:24*)
7. What two prophets did Jesus talk about? (*Elijah and Elisha, Luke 4:25-27*)
8. How did the people in the synagogue feel? (*angry, Luke 4:28*)
9. What did the people want to do to Jesus? (*throw Him off a cliff, Luke 4:29*)

Say • *What is the good news about Jesus? Jesus died for our sins.*

If you choose to review with boys and girls how to become a Christian, explain that kids are welcome to speak with you or another teacher if they have questions.

- **God rules.** God created and is in charge of everything. (Gen. 1:1; Rev. 4:11; Col. 1:16-17)
- **We sinned.** Since Adam and Eve, everyone has chosen to disobey God. (Rom. 3:23; 6:23)
- **God provided.** God sent His Son, Jesus, to rescue

us from the punishment we deserve. (John 3:16; Eph. 2:8-9)

- **Jesus gives.** Jesus lived a perfect life, died on the cross for our sins, and rose again so we can be welcomed into God's family. (Rom. 5:8; 2 Cor. 5:21; 1 Pet. 3:18)
- **We respond.** Believe that Jesus alone saves you. Repent. Tell God that your faith is in Jesus. (Rom. 10:9-10,13)

• Gospel Plan Poster (enhanced CD)

Activity choice (10 minutes)

Option 1: Shout it out!

Form five groups of kids. If your group is small, kids may work individually or in pairs. Assign each group one of the key statements from the gospel plan poster.

Encourage each group to create motions for their assigned statement. If kids struggle, suggest the following motions:

1. God rules. [*Hold hands to side of head like positioning a crown.*]
2. We sinned. [*Kneel down and cover hands with face.*]
3. God provided. [*Hold palms up in front of body as if offering a gift.*]
4. Jesus gives. [*Stretch arms outward to form the shape of a cross.*]
5. We respond. [*Fold hands and bow head as if praying.*]

After several minutes, invite each group to share its motions and shout its assigned statement. Explain that the gospel is good news! It is God's plan for saving people from sin. We can share the gospel with others and pray that they would trust in Jesus as Lord and Savior.

Say • *What is the good news about Jesus? Jesus died for our sins.*

Option 2: *Welcome* hunt

Write the letters *W-E-L-C-O-M-E* on separate sticky notes. Prior to small group, place the sticky notes on small, random objects throughout the room. Invite kids to hunt for letters. Explain that there are seven letters scattered around the room. When a kid finds an object marked with a letter, he should bring that object to the center of the room.

After kids locate all seven letters, challenge them to work together to rearrange the letters to spell a word. (*welcome*) Ask kids to share some ways they can make others feel welcome in their homes or at church.

Say • Jesus was not welcome in His hometown of Nazareth, but He welcomes us into God's family. Jesus will never turn away anyone who comes to Him. (John 6:37) Jesus gives eternal life to those who trust in Him, and believers will live with Him forever in heaven.

• We can welcome others into our homes, church, and classrooms. We can share with them the gospel—the good news about Jesus. *What is the good news about Jesus? Jesus died for our sins.*

Journal and prayer (5 minutes)

Say • Draw in your journal a picture of your hometown, or write about some of your favorite memories in that town.

Invite kids to share prayer requests. Close the group in prayer, thanking Jesus for welcoming everyone into God's family even though people rejected Jesus. As time allows, lead kids to complete the activity page "Crack the Code."

Margin materials list:
- sticky notes
- marker

- pencils
- journals
- Journal Page, 1 per kid (enhanced CD)
- "Crack the Code" activity page, 1 per kid

Unit 26: JESUS PERFORMED MIRACLES

Big Picture Questions

Session 1:
What happened when Jesus performed miracles? Jesus' miracles helped people believe in Him.

Session 2:
What did the evil spirit know about Jesus? Jesus is the Holy One of God.

Session 3:
How can we show we are thankful to Jesus? We can serve Jesus and live for Him.

Session 4:
Who can take away our sin? Jesus can and wants to cleanse us from sin.

Session 5:
How could Jesus forgive people's sins? Jesus was going to take the punishment for sin when He died on the cross.

Session 6:
What did Jesus' miracles prove? Jesus' miracles proved that He is the Son of God.

Unit 26: JESUS PERFORMED MIRACLES

Unit Description: Jesus' miracles are one of the main ways God brought people to faith in Him. Jesus demonstrated His power and authority when He healed the sick and set free those held captive by sin. Many people who saw His signs followed Jesus and believed that He is the Messiah, the Son of God.

Unit Key Passage:
John 20:30-31

Unit Christ Connection:
Jesus' miracles demonstrated His divine authority.

Session 1:
Jesus Healed an Official's Son
John 4:46-54

Session 2:
Jesus Drove Out Evil Spirits
Mark 1:21-28; Luke 4:31-37

Session 3:
Jesus Healed Peter's Mother-in-Law
Matthew 8:14-17; Mark 1:29-31; Luke 4:38-39

Session 4:
Jesus Cleansed a Leper
Matthew 8:1-4; Mark 1:40-45; Luke 5:12-16

Session 5:
Four Friends Helped
Matthew 9:1-8; Mark 2:1-12; Luke 5:17-26

Session 6:
Jesus Healed a Man's Hand
Matthew 12:9-14; Mark 3:1-6; Luke 6:6-11

Leader BIBLE STUDY

Jesus entered Galilee after traveling through Samaria. The Galileans had seen Jesus in Jerusalem at the Passover feast, and they welcomed Him. Jesus went to the town of Cana, where He had performed His first miracle—turning water into wine. News spread of Jesus' whereabouts, and an official hurried to find Him.

The official's son was sick in Capernaum, about 20 miles away. The boy was so sick, the official knew he would die if he didn't get help. So the official went to Jesus. Imagine the urgency in his voice when he pleaded for Jesus to come heal his son.

But Jesus didn't rush away to Capernaum. Instead, He challenged the official and the Galileans: "You people must see miracles and signs before you believe in Me."

It was true; many people who saw Jesus' miracles followed Him and believed in Him. (See John 2:11,23; 3:2; 6:2,14; 12:11,18.) Jesus was willing to help people, but He didn't want them to miss the point. The miracles were great, but Jesus had come to offer something greater. The miracles were signs that pointed to who Jesus is: the Son of God who offers eternal life.

The official pleaded again, "Sir, come down before my boy dies!" Jesus answered, "Go. Your son will live." The official believed what Jesus said. He headed home, and his servants confirmed the truth: His son was well. The fever had left him at the same time Jesus said, "Your son will live." So the official and everyone in his household believed in Jesus.

Jesus' miracles are one of the main ways God brought people to faith in Him. Jesus demonstrated His power and authority when He healed the sick and set captives free. Jesus performed more miracles than the apostle John recorded. John concludes his Gospel by explaining that "these are written so that you may believe Jesus is the Messiah, the Son of God, and by believing you may have life in His name" (John 20:31).

Older Kids BIBLE STUDY OVERVIEW

Session Title: Jesus Healed an Official's Son
Bible Passage: John 4:46-54
Big Picture Question: What happened when Jesus performed miracles?
Jesus' miracles helped people believe in Him.
Key Passage: John 20:30-31
Unit Christ Connection: Jesus' miracles demonstrated His divine
authority.

Small Group Opening

Large Group Leader

Small Group Leader

The BIBLE STORY

Jesus Healed an Official's Son
John 4:46-54

After spending time in the city of Jerusalem for the Passover feast, Jesus traveled north to Galilee. On the way, He stopped in Samaria, where He met a Samaritan woman at a well. Then Jesus went to His hometown of Nazareth, where the people rejected Him. Now **Jesus went to Cana (KAY nuh), a city in Galilee.** Jesus had been there before; Cana was the place where Jesus had performed His first miracle.

At this time, a man living several miles away needed Jesus' help. The man was one of the king's important officials, and his son was very sick. When the official heard that Jesus had come to the region of Galilee, he went to see Him.

The official begged Jesus, "Please come heal my son; he is about to die!"

Jesus answered the man, "You and everyone else in Galilee must see miracles before you will believe in Me."

Jesus healed people so they would see that He is God's Son and believe in Him as the promised Savior.

The official begged again. "Sir," he said, "please come before my boy dies."

Jesus answered, "Go. Your son will live."

The man believed that Jesus was telling the truth. He trusted that Jesus had healed his son, even though the boy was several miles away. Jesus' power to heal was not limited by distance.

The man started his journey back home, eager to be with his son again. **Before he even got there, his servants rushed out to meet him. They had great news!**

"Your son is alive!" they said. "He is not sick anymore!"

"What time did he get better?" the official asked. The servants told him the exact hour that the boy's fever went away. The official realized that his son had gotten better at the same time Jesus had said, "Your son will live." The man believed in Jesus, and so did everyone in his household.

This was the second miraculous sign that Jesus did after He traveled from Judea up to Galilee.

Christ Connection: The official wanted Jesus to save his son from death, and it was not until Jesus did so that he understood who Jesus is: the promised Messiah. It took faith for the official to believe Jesus' words— that his son was healed. In healing the official's son, Jesus showed His authority and power as God's Son.

Small Group OPENING

Session Title: Jesus Healed an Official's Son
Bible Passage: John 4:46-54
Big Picture Question: What happened when Jesus performed miracles?
Jesus' miracles helped people believe in Him.
Key Passage: John 20:30-31
Unit Christ Connection: Jesus' miracles demonstrated His divine
authority.

Welcome time

Greet each kid as he or she arrives. Use this time to collect
the offering, fill out attendance sheets, and help new kids
connect to your group. Lead a few volunteers to share about
a time they were sick. Ask each volunteer how many days
she was sick. Did she see a doctor to get better?

Activity page (5 minutes)

• "Right On Time"
activity page,
1 per kid
• pencils

Distribute the "Right On Time" activity page to each kid.
Instruct kids to find the clock that matches each time listed
below the blanks. When kids make a match, they should
write the letter on the clock in the corresponding blank.

Challenge them to solve the code to figure out what
Jesus did to help people believe in Him. (*miracles*) Be
prepared to assist any kids who struggle to tell time.

Say • Does anyone know any of the miracles Jesus did?
Jesus performed many miracles. We will hear about
one of them in today's Bible story.

Session starter (10 minutes)

Option 1: Tell the truth
Guide kids to sit down. Explain that you will read a

statement. If a kid believes the statement is true, she should stand. If she believes the statement is false, she should remain seated.

- Jupiter is the largest planet in our solar system. (*true*)
- The brown pelican is the state bird of Louisiana. (*true*)
- The state of Florida is larger than the country of England. (*true*)
- The eye of an ostrich is larger than its brain. (*true*)
- People typically spend more than two hours each night dreaming. (*true*)
- A quarter has 119 grooves on its edge. (*true*)

Say • How do you know if someone is telling the truth? Today we are going to hear a Bible story about a man who trusted that Jesus was telling the truth.

Option 2: One day, I will …

• numbered cube

Invite kids to take turns rolling a numbered cube. Each player should complete the following statement based on the number he rolled: "One day, I will … "

For example, a player who rolls a *3* should state three things he will do in the future. Encourage kids to consider things they plan to do later today, next week, next year, or in five years.

Say • We can make plans for the future, but they won't always happen. God knows the future. In today's Bible story, Jesus told a man about his son's future. What Jesus said would happen did happen! Jesus' words are always true.

Transition to large group

Large Group LEADER

Session Title: Jesus Healed an Official's Son
Bible Passage: John 4:46-54
Big Picture Question: What happened when Jesus performed miracles?
Jesus' miracles helped people believe in Him.
Key Passage: John 20:30-31
Unit Christ Connection: Jesus' miracles demonstrated His divine
authority.

• room decorations

Tip: Select
decorations that fit
your ministry and
budget.

Suggested Theme Decorating Ideas: Create a backdrop
to look like a trophy case or hall of fame. Cut yellow paper
to resemble trophies and hang a pennant banner. Position
various sports equipment to the side such as basketballs,
baseballs, baseball gloves and bats, swim goggles, running
shoes, tennis rackets, and so forth.

Countdown

• countdown video

Show the countdown video as your kids arrive, and set it to
end as large group time begins.

Introduce the session (3 minutes)

• leader attire

*[Large Group Leader enters wearing a ball cap and
baseball glove. Leader punches his or her hand into the
glove.]*

Leader •OK! All right! I'm glad you are all here! Whew,
my name is [*your name*], and I just finished my first
baseball practice of the season. I think the coach might let
me play third base. I'm so excited.

Anyway, I'm not here to tell you about baseball today. I
came to tell you about something even more exciting than
a home run or a double play. I came to tell you a story
about something that really happened—a miracle! Let's

check out this timeline map to see which Bible story we will hear today.

Timeline map (1 minute)

• Timeline Map

Leader • This timeline map helps us see the big picture of the Bible—from the creation of the world to the time in the future when Jesus will come back and be King over everything. Today we are going to look at something that happened when Jesus, God's Son, was on earth. Before Jesus died on the cross, He spent three years teaching people about God. He even performed miracles. Today's Bible story is called "Jesus Healed an Official's Son."

Big picture question (1 minute)

Leader • Speaking of miracles, let's think about our big picture question. We will have a big picture question each week. Will you listen to the Bible story to help me find the answer? Great! Today's big picture question is, *What happened when Jesus performed miracles?*

Hmm. I guess you don't witness a miracle and just do nothing. When people saw Jesus' miracles, something happened. Let's listen to the Bible story to find out what.

Tell the Bible story (10 minutes)

• "Jesus Healed an Official's Son" video
• Bibles, 1 per kid
• Bible Story Picture Slide or Poster
• Big Picture Question Slide or Poster

Open your Bible to John 4:46-54 and tell the Bible story in your own words, or show the Bible story video "Jesus Healed an Official's Son."

Leader • Jesus was in a town called Cana (KAY nuh). A royal official heard about Jesus, and he traveled several miles to ask Jesus for help. You see, the official's son was very sick. The official had probably done everything he could think of to help his son. He probably took him to the doctor, but his son was not getting better. The official

Jesus Performed Miracles   **79**

Tip: A Bible story script is provided at the beginning of every session. You may use it to guide you as you prepare to teach the Bible story in your own words. For a shorter version of the Bible story, read only the bolded text.

was certain his son would die.

So the official begged Jesus to come heal his son. If anyone could help the boy, it was Jesus. But Jesus did not go with the man. He did not place His hands on the boy to make him well. What did Jesus do?

Jesus said, "Go. Your son will live."

The man believed Jesus! He did not beg Jesus to go home with him and prove that his son was OK. The official trusted that Jesus had the power to heal his son, even from several miles away.

So the man hurried home, and before he even got there, his servants ran to meet him. They told the man that his son wasn't sick anymore! And he had gotten better at the same time Jesus said, "Your son will live." It was a miracle!

The official and everyone in his household believed in Jesus. So, **what happened when Jesus performed miracles? Jesus' miracles helped people believe in Him.** That's our big picture question and answer. Say it with me. **What happened when Jesus performed miracles? Jesus' miracles helped people believe in Him.**

Jesus is the Messiah God promised to send. He is God's Son, and He is powerful. The official had faith; he believed without seeing proof. We can have faith too. We can believe that Jesus is Lord and Savior, and we can trust Him to rescue us from our sins.

The Gospel: God's Plan for Me (optional)

• Bible

Using Scripture and the guide provided, explain to boys and girls how to become a Christian. Tell kids how they can respond, and provide counselors to speak with each kid individually. Guide counselors to use open-ended questions to allow kids to determine the direction of the conversation.

Encourage boys and girls to ask their parents, small group leaders, or other adults any questions they may have about becoming a Christian.

Key passage (5 minutes)

- Key Passage Slide or Poster
- "Written" song

Leader • Does anyone know why the Bible includes stories about Jesus' miracles? Why is it important for us to know about Jesus healing an official's son? Our key passage has the answer.

Guide kids to open their Bibles to John 20:30-31. Choose a volunteer to read the passage aloud.

Leader • The Bible says that Jesus' miraculous signs were written down so that we can read about them and believe that Jesus is the Christ, the Son of God, and that by believing we may have life. When we trust in Jesus as Lord and Savior, He gives us eternal life.

Sing the key passage song "Written."

Discussion starter video (5 minutes)

- "Unit 26 Session 1" discussion starter video

Leader • If someone says something is going to happen, do you believe it? Watch this video.

Show the "Unit 26 Session 1" video.

Leader • Not everything we say we will do will actually happen. Only God knows the future. But Jesus is God's Son, and when Jesus said that the official's boy would live, the official trusted that Jesus was telling the truth.

Jesus performed a miracle by healing the boy. ***What happened when Jesus performed miracles? Jesus' miracles helped people believe in Him.***

Sing (3 minutes)

- "This Is Amazing Grace" song

Leader • Jesus was so kind to help people. God sent Jesus to earth to help people, not just people who were sick or injured, but sinners—people who are separated from God because they disobey Him. Jesus took the punishment we deserve for our sin by dying on the cross. When we trust in Him, we can be with God forever in heaven. That's worth singing about! Sing our theme song with me.

Lead boys and girls to sing "This Is Amazing Grace."

Prayer (2 minutes)

Leader • Before you go to your small groups, let's pray.

Lord God, Your grace is amazing. You are so kind to us, and You give us good gifts that we do not deserve. We praise You for Jesus' miraculous acts, and we know that He is the promised Messiah. God, thank You for today and for Your Word. Go with us and remind us of the good news about Jesus. Amen.

Dismiss to small groups

The Gospel: God's Plan for Me

Ask kids if they have ever heard the word *gospel*. Clarify that the word *gospel* means "good news." It is the message about Christ, the kingdom of God, and salvation. Use the following guide to share the gospel with kids.

God rules. Explain to kids that the Bible tells us God created everything, and He is in charge of everything. Invite a volunteer to read Genesis 1:1 from the Bible. Read Revelation 4:11 or Colossians 1:16-17 aloud and explain what these verses mean.

We sinned. Tell kids that since the time of Adam and Eve, everyone has chosen to disobey God. (Romans 3:23) The Bible calls this sin. Because God is holy, God cannot be around sin. Sin separates us from God and deserves God's punishment of death. (Romans 6:23)

God provided. Choose a child to read John 3:16 aloud. Say that God sent His Son, Jesus, the perfect solution to our sin problem, to rescue us from the punishment we deserve. It's something we, as sinners, could never earn on our own. Jesus alone saves us. Read and explain Ephesians 2:8-9.

Jesus gives. Share with kids that Jesus lived a perfect life, died on the cross for our sins, and rose again. Because Jesus gave up His life for us, we can be welcomed into God's family for eternity. This is the best gift ever! Read Romans 5:8; 2 Corinthians 5:21; or 1 Peter 3:18.

We respond. Tell kids that they can respond to Jesus. Read Romans 10:9-10,13. Review these aspects of our response: Believe in your heart that Jesus alone saves you through what He's already done on the cross. Repent, turning from self and sin to Jesus. Tell God and others that your faith is in Jesus.

Offer to talk with any child who is interested in responding to Jesus.

Small Group LEADER

Session Title: Jesus Healed an Official's Son
Bible Passage: John 4:46-54
Big Picture Question: What happened when Jesus performed miracles?
Jesus' miracles helped people believe in Him.
Key Passage: John 20:30-31
Unit Christ Connection: Jesus' miracles demonstrated His divine
authority.

Key passage activity (5 minutes)

• Key Passage Poster

Invite kids to work together to create motions for key words
in the Bible passage. Kids can perform the motions to
help them memorize John 20:30-31. Encourage kids to be
creative. Be prepared to give suggestions if kids need help
making up motions or choosing key words.

Lead kids to practice their motions as they say the key
passage together several times.

Say • Excellent job! You can use these motions to help
you memorize this passage. Remember, the apostle
John wrote about Jesus' miracles in his Gospel for
a reason. Why? So that people would read about the
things Jesus did and believe that He is the Son of
God, and by believing in Him that they may have
eternal life.

Bible story review & Bible skills (10 minutes)

• Bibles, 1 per kid
• Small Group Visual Pack
• ball
• "This Is Amazing Grace" song (optional)

Provide a Bible for each kid and instruct kids to stand.
Guide them to find the Book of John in the Bible. When a
kid has located the book, she may sit down. Assist any kids
who need help. Ask kids if the Book of John is in the Old
Testament or New Testament. (*New Testament*)

Review the timeline in the small group visual pack. Retell or review the Bible story in your own words or use the bolded text of the Bible story script.

Instruct kids to stand in a circle. Give one kid a ball and invite kids to gently toss the ball around the circle. Play music in the background as kids play. When you stop the music, the kid holding the ball or the last kid to touch the ball must answer a review question. Then restart the music and play another round.

1. What city did Jesus travel to? (*Cana in Galilee, John 4:46*)
2. Who was sick and needed Jesus' help? (*a royal official's son, John 4:46-47*)
3. What did Jesus say the people needed to see to believe in Jesus? (*miracles, signs and wonders; John 4:48*)
4. What did Jesus say to the man? (*"Go, your son will live"; John 4:50*)
5. Who met the man on his way home? (*his servants, John 4:51*)
6. What did the servants say about the man's son? (*the boy was alive, John 4:51*)
7. Who healed the official's son? (*Jesus healed him, John 4:52-53*)
8. **What happened when Jesus performed miracles? Jesus' miracles helped people believe in Him.**

If you choose to review with boys and girls how to become a Christian, explain that kids are welcome to speak with you or another teacher if they have questions.

- **God rules.** God created and is in charge of everything. (Gen. 1:1; Rev. 4:11; Col. 1:16-17)
- **We sinned.** Since Adam and Eve, everyone has chosen to disobey God. (Rom. 3:23; 6:23)
- **God provided.** God sent His Son, Jesus, to rescue

us from the punishment we deserve. (John 3:16; Eph. 2:8-9)

- **Jesus gives.** Jesus lived a perfect life, died on the cross for our sins, and rose again so we can be welcomed into God's family. (Rom. 5:8; 2 Cor. 5:21; 1 Pet. 3:18)
- **We respond.** Believe that Jesus alone saves you. Repent. Tell God that your faith is in Jesus. (Rom. 10:9-10,13)

Activity choice (10 minutes)

- index cards
- marker

Option 1: Career charades

Write several career titles on separate index cards. Consider preparing one card per kid. (Suggestions: chef, professional football player, dentist, artist, mechanic, waiter or waitress, farmer, firefighter, teacher, musician, nurse, pilot, news reporter, and so forth)

Hold the cards facedown. Choose a volunteer to select a card. The volunteer must act out the profession. She may not speak or make sounds. The other kids will guess what career the volunteer is acting out. When kids guess the volunteer's career, choose another volunteer to select a card. Play several rounds as time allows.

Say • How did you know what career card the volunteer had chosen? You could tell who the volunteer was by what he did. Jesus' miracles showed people that He is the Messiah. *What happened when Jesus performed miracles? Jesus' miracles helped people believe in Him.*

- plastic spoons, 1 per kid
- red, yellow, and green chocolate-coated candy pieces

Option 2: Pass and play

Direct kids to stand in a circle. Give each kid a plastic spoon. Position one chocolate-coated candy piece on the spoons of three players not standing next to each other. When you say go, players should begin passing the candy pieces to the right, one player at a time. Encourage kids to be careful not to drop the candy pieces.

At random intervals, call for kids to stop. First, give a review task to the player holding the green candy piece. Then instruct kids to begin again. When you call for kids to stop a second time, give a review task to the player holding the yellow candy piece. Begin again, and then call stop. Give a review task to the player holding the red candy piece. Continue playing, pausing and challenging players holding specific candy pieces to provide an answer.

- Green: Name a person in the Bible story. (*royal official, Jesus, official's son, official's servants*)
- Yellow: Briefly retell the Bible story in your own words.
- Red: Say the big picture question and answer.

Journal and prayer (5 minutes)

- pencils
- journals
- Bibles
- Journal Page, 1 per kid (enhanced CD)
- "Mysterious Miracles" activity page, 1 per kid

Read a few of the following passages aloud: Matt. 17:14-20; Mark 10:13-16; Luke 8:40-42,49-55; John 4:46-54. Prompt kids to think about what these verses say about Jesus.

Say • How does Jesus feel about kids? Write in your journals how these verses make you feel. You may also draw pictures if you would like.

Invite kids to share prayer requests. Close the group in prayer, or allow a volunteer to close the group in prayer.

As time allows, lead kids to complete the activity page "Mysterious Miracles." Encourage them to think of questions they have about miracles that begin with *Who? What? When? Where? Why?* and *How?*

Leader BIBLE STUDY

During His ministry, Jesus demonstrated His power and authority through miracles. Among Jesus' healing miracles, Jesus drove out demons, or unclean spirits. Demons are evil angels—created, spiritual beings—who sinned against God. The Bible identifies Satan as the head of the demons. (See Job 1:6.)

Demons are enemies of God. They oppose God's work and try to turn people away from God and the gospel. When Jesus was preaching at the synagogue in Capernaum, an unclean spirit began to shout through a man. Jesus commanded the spirit to be quiet, and He drove the demon away.

Jesus' power over demons marked the launch of God's kingdom. When Jesus cast a demon out of a man who was blind and mute, He said, "If I drive out demons by the Spirit of God, then the kingdom of God has come to you" (Matt. 12:28).

Still today, demons try all sorts of strategies to keep believers from being effective witnesses for Christ, including doubt, temptation, pride, guilt, and fear. But we do not need to fear demons because Jesus gives believers authority over them. In the New Testament, Jesus gave His disciples authority over demons, and the demons submitted to them when they commanded them in Christ's name. (See Luke 9:1; 10:17,19; Acts 8:7; 16:18.)

Jesus said that Satan is "the father of lies" (John 8:44), and he is the accuser (Rev. 12:10). Satan's goal is to turn people away from God. When Satan accuses us as guilty before the Judge, he is right; our sin makes us guilty. But he leaves out the gospel: Jesus died for our sin. He took the punishment we deserve.

When Jesus died on the cross, He defeated Satan. (See Heb. 2:14-15.) One day Satan will be cast out forever. (Rev. 20:10)

Older Kids BIBLE STUDY OVERVIEW

Session Title: Jesus Drove Out Evil Spirits
Bible Passage: Mark 1:21-28; Luke 4:31-37
Big Picture Question: What did the evil spirit know about Jesus? Jesus is the Holy One of God.
Key Passage: John 20:30-31
Unit Christ Connection: Jesus' miracles demonstrated His divine authority.

Small Group Opening

Large Group Leader

Small Group Leader

The BIBLE STORY

Jesus Drove Out Evil Spirits
Mark 1:21-28; Luke 4:31-37

Jesus was an adult when His ministry began. The people who saw Jesus and heard Him talk did not know right away who He was. They did not realize that He was the Messiah God had promised. They did not know that Jesus had come to save people from sin. Jesus spent three years performing miracles and teaching people about God and His kingdom.

One day, Jesus and His followers went to Capernaum (kuh PUHR nay uhm). Capernaum was a town in Galilee, near the sea. On the Sabbath day, Jesus went into the synagogue. The Sabbath was a special day when the Jews rested from their work and worshiped God. They went to the synagogue to learn about God's laws.

That day, Jesus began teaching the people in the synagogue. Everyone was amazed! They had heard other men teach about the law before, but Jesus was not like the other men. He taught with authority, like He really knew what He was talking about.

All of a sudden, a man started shouting. Something was wrong with him; he was not himself. **The man had an evil spirit inside him,** and the spirit was from the Devil.

"What do You want with us, Jesus of Nazareth?" The man shouted, but it was the evil spirit inside of him that was talking. "Did You come here to destroy us? I know who You are; You are the Holy One of God!"

Jesus warned the evil spirit to stop. **"Be quiet, and come out of him!" Jesus commanded. The evil spirit** caused the man to fall to the ground, and the man started shaking. Then he shouted, and the spirit **came out. The man was not hurt.**

Everyone who saw what had happened was amazed. They began asking each other questions, like "What's going on?" **They had never seen someone like Jesus before.** The people knew Jesus was different because when He commanded the evil spirit to come out of the man, the spirit obeyed Him.

The news about Jesus spread quickly. People started talking about Him and what He had said and done. Soon many people in Galilee had heard about Him.

Christ Connection: Jesus is the King who has come to make all things right. By commanding the evil spirit to come out of the man, Jesus showed He has power over all our enemies. One day Jesus will take away Satan, sin, and death once and for all.

Small Group OPENING

Session Title: Jesus Drove Out Evil Spirits
Bible Passage: Mark 1:21-28; Luke 4:31-37
Big Picture Question: What did the evil spirit know about Jesus? Jesus is the Holy One of God.
Key Passage: John 20:30-31
Unit Christ Connection: Jesus' miracles demonstrated His divine authority.

Welcome time

Greet each kid as he or she arrives. Use this time to collect the offering, fill out attendance sheets, and help new kids connect to your group. Prompt kids to imagine meeting the president or other leader. What question would they ask?

Activity page (5 minutes)

- "Jesus Said It" activity page, 1 per kid
- pencils

Give each kid a "Jesus Said It" activity page. Direct each kid to put his finger on the box that says *Jesus*. Read the instructions aloud, one at a time, as kids follow along. Pause after each clue so kids can write the next word in the blank. When you finish reading all the clues, kids should have written something Jesus said in today's Bible story. (*Jesus said, "Be quiet and come out of him."*)

Say • Jesus said these words in today's Bible story. I wonder who He was talking to and why He said that. We will have to listen carefully to the Bible story to find out.

Session starter (10 minutes)

Option 1: Greater and less

Form two teams of kids. Instruct each team to sit together.

Explain that teams will take turns. You will name a person or an animal, and the team must name a person or animal that is greater and explain why.

For example, if you say, "Mouse," kids might respond, "Cat. Cats eat mice." If you say, "Hippopotamus," kids might say, "Dog. Dogs make better pets." Remember, a creative answer may be correct if kids can explain why. (Suggestions: chicken, ostrich, bear, mayor, student, athlete)

Say • No one is greater than Jesus. He has power over all things. In today's Bible story, we will hear how Jesus showed His power one day at the synagogue.

Option 2: Pardon the interruption

• bell or whistle

Guide kids to stand or sit in a circle. Choose one player to begin. Kids will take turns telling a story. If necessary, provide a prompt such as "Tell us about a boy who dreamed of traveling to the moon," or "Tell us about a girl who won a lifetime supply of chocolate."

The first player should begin telling the story. After several seconds, ring a bell or blow a whistle. The first player should stop talking and the player to her right should pick up telling the story where she left off.

Continue interrupting the speaker at random intervals and lead the next player to begin. Play for several minutes, giving everyone a chance to contribute to the story.

Say • You are so creative! Were you ever frustrated when I interrupted you? Today we are going to hear a Bible story about a time Jesus was interrupted. Jesus was speaking in the synagogue when a man began shouting. We'll find out what Jesus did next.

Transition to large group

Large Group LEADER

Session Title: Jesus Drove Out Evil Spirits
Bible Passage: Mark 1:21-28; Luke 4:31-37
Big Picture Question: What did the evil spirit know about Jesus? Jesus is the Holy One of God.
Key Passage: John 20:30-31
Unit Christ Connection: Jesus' miracles demonstrated His divine authority.

Countdown

• countdown video

Show the countdown video as your kids arrive, and set it to end as large group time begins.

Introduce the session (3 minutes)

• leader attire
• large foam or inflatable ball

[Large Group Leader enters wearing a button-down shirt, khaki pants, and bowling shoes. Leader carries a large foam or inflatable ball resembling a bowling ball.]

Leader • Hi, everyone! It's me, [*your name*]. Thanks for coming. Well, you might be wondering where my baseball uniform is. Unfortunately, I am not playing baseball anymore. My coach put me on third base, and I was not very good at it. Then, halfway through practice, I started sneezing and my eyes got all itchy … I think I am allergic to something outdoors.

So this week, I tried bowling. Bowling is fun! [*Act out bowling.*] You hold the ball like this, swing it back, and … yes! Strike! Well, I know you are not here to listen to my bowling stories. Let's get started learning about the Bible!

Timeline map (1 minute)

• Timeline Map

Use the timeline map to point out and review the previous

Bible story, "Jesus Healed an Official's Son."

Leader • See here? Last time, we heard about a royal official whose son was very sick. Jesus performed a miracle; He healed the boy, even from several miles away! When the official saw that his boy was better, he and everyone in his house believed in Jesus. Do you remember the big picture question from last time? *What happened when Jesus performed miracles? Jesus' miracles helped people believe in Him.*

Today's Bible story is about another time Jesus helped a man in need. This Bible story is called "Jesus Drove Out Evil Spirits." Wow, that sounds serious.

Big picture question (1 minute)

Leader • Jesus drove out evil spirits more than once, but today we are going to hear about one time that Jesus drove out an evil spirit when He was in the synagogue. This evil spirit interrupted Jesus when He was teaching, and it said something about Jesus that was true. I wonder what the evil spirit knew about Jesus. Actually, that's our big picture question: *What did the evil spirit know about Jesus?* Listen carefully to the Bible story to find the answer.

Tell the Bible story (10 minutes)

- "Jesus Drove Out Evil Spirits" video
- Bibles, 1 per kid
- Bible Story Picture Slide or Poster
- Big Picture Question Slide or Poster

Open your Bible to Mark 1:21-28 or Luke 4:31-37. Tell the Bible story in your own words, or show the Bible story video "Jesus Drove Out Evil Spirits."

Leader • Jesus went to the synagogue to teach on the Sabbath. People came to learn about God's laws. When the people heard Jesus speak, they knew He was different from other teachers. Jesus taught with authority.

While Jesus was teaching, a man interrupted Him. The

man was shouting because he had an evil spirit inside him. The evil spirit knew who Jesus is, and it said to Jesus, "What do You want with us, Jesus? Did You come here to destroy us? I know who You are; You are the Holy One of God!"

The evil spirit was right. Jesus had come to destroy evil. Jesus had come to earth to rescue people from sin, and He was going to defeat sin and Satan and death once and for all. Jesus told the evil spirit to be quiet and to come out of the man. The evil spirit obeyed Jesus. Jesus has power over evil.

Did you hear the answer to our big picture question? *What did the evil spirit know about Jesus? Jesus is the Holy One of God.* Say that with me. *What did the evil spirit know about Jesus? Jesus is the Holy One of God.*

The people in the synagogue saw what happened, and they could hardly believe it! They had never met anyone like Jesus before. The people began talking about Jesus, and news about Jesus spread throughout the land.

Wow, Jesus is more powerful than all our enemies! When He tells evil spirits what to do, they obey Him! Evil still affects our world today, but Jesus is King and one day He will come back and take away Satan, sin, and death once and for all.

The Gospel: God's Plan for Me (optional)

• Bible

Using Scripture and the guide provided, explain to boys and girls how to become a Christian. Tell kids how they can respond, and provide counselors to speak with each kid individually. Encourage boys and girls to ask their parents, small group leaders, or other adults any questions they may have about becoming a Christian.

Key passage (5 minutes)

• Key Passage Slide or
Poster
• "Written" song

Leader • Does anyone remember our key passage? It's
John 20:30-31. Let's read it together.

Guide kids to find John 20:30-31 in their Bibles. Display
the key passage poster and lead kids to read the passage
aloud.

Leader • These verses are in the Book of John. John wrote
down many of the miraculous signs Jesus did. Did John
write down *all* of them? No! The Bible says that Jesus
performed many other signs that are not written in the
Bible. Wow!

Let's say the key passage again. See if you can
memorize these verses over the next few weeks.

Choose a couple volunteers to lead the group in singing
"Written."

Discussion starter video (5 minutes)

• "Unit 26 Session 2"
discussion starter
video

Leader • What do you do when you see something
amazing? Don't you want to tell everyone about it? Let's
watch this video.

Show the "Unit 26 Session 2" video.

Leader • Tell me some amazing things you've seen
recently. In today's Bible story, all the people in the
synagogue saw Jesus command the evil spirit to come out
of the man, and the evil spirit obeyed Jesus. The people
were amazed, and they told others what they saw. Soon
the news about Jesus had spread all over the city.

Sing (3 minutes)

• "This Is Amazing
Grace" song

Leader • We saw in the Bible story that Jesus has power
over all our enemies. Jesus has authority over everything.
[*See Matt. 28:18.*] He is King. It's amazing that Jesus left
His place in heaven to come to earth and rescue sinners.

He came to give us grace—favor we do not deserve. He died on the cross for our sins. Let's praise Him.

Lead boys and girls to sing "This Is Amazing Grace."

Prayer (2 minutes)

Leader • *What did the evil spirit know about Jesus? Jesus is the Holy One of God.* The evil spirit knew who Jesus is, but the evil spirit did not love Jesus. The Devil and the evil spirits are enemies of God; they are against everything God loves, including His own Son. Before you go to your small groups, let's pray.

God, thank You for sending Jesus to rescue us from our sins. Thank You for giving Him power over all things, even evil things. We know that Jesus is the Holy One of God, and He deserves our praise. Help us to trust in Your goodness and that You are in control of all things. We love You. Amen.

Dismiss to small groups

The Gospel: God's Plan for Me

Ask kids if they have ever heard the word *gospel*. Clarify that the word *gospel* means "good news." It is the message about Christ, the kingdom of God, and salvation. Use the following guide to share the gospel with kids.

God rules. Explain to kids that the Bible tells us God created everything, and He is in charge of everything. Invite a volunteer to read Genesis 1:1 from the Bible. Read Revelation 4:11 or Colossians 1:16-17 aloud and explain what these verses mean.

We sinned. Tell kids that since the time of Adam and Eve, everyone has chosen to disobey God. (Romans 3:23) The Bible calls this sin. Because God is holy, God cannot be around sin. Sin separates us from God and deserves God's punishment of death. (Romans 6:23)

God provided. Choose a child to read John 3:16 aloud. Say that God sent His Son, Jesus, the perfect solution to our sin problem, to rescue us from the punishment we deserve. It's something we, as sinners, could never earn on our own. Jesus alone saves us. Read and explain Ephesians 2:8-9.

Jesus gives. Share with kids that Jesus lived a perfect life, died on the cross for our sins, and rose again. Because Jesus gave up His life for us, we can be welcomed into God's family for eternity. This is the best gift ever! Read Romans 5:8; 2 Corinthians 5:21; or 1 Peter 3:18.

We respond. Tell kids that they can respond to Jesus. Read Romans 10:9-10,13. Review these aspects of our response: Believe in your heart that Jesus alone saves you through what He's already done on the cross. Repent, turning from self and sin to Jesus. Tell God and others that your faith is in Jesus.

Offer to talk with any child who is interested in responding to Jesus.

Small Group LEADER

Session Title: Jesus Drove Out Evil Spirits
Bible Passage: Mark 1:21-28; Luke 4:31-37
Big Picture Question: What did the evil spirit know about Jesus? Jesus is the Holy One of God.
Key Passage: John 20:30-31
Unit Christ Connection: Jesus' miracles demonstrated His divine authority.

Key passage activity (5 minutes)

• Key Passage Poster
• paper plates, 1 per kid
• marker

Write words or phrases of the key passage on separate paper plates. Prepare one plate per kid.

Invite kids to sit around a table or in a circle on the floor. Mix up the paper plates and give each kid one plate. Kids should work together and pass their plates to other players until the plates are in the correct order. When kids finish rearranging the plates, lead them to say the key passage together. For a more active game, direct kids to hold their paper plates and rearrange themselves until the plates are in the correct order. If time allows, mix up the plates and redistribute them to play again.

Say • Well done! Can someone tell me why the Bible has these stories about Jesus' miracles? Yes. Reading about the miraculous signs Jesus did helps us believe that He is the Son of God. Those who believe in Him as Lord and Savior will have eternal life.

Bible story review & Bible skills (10 minutes)

• Bibles, 1 per kid
• Small Group Visual Pack

Review the timeline in the small group visual pack. Retell or review the Bible story in your own words or use the bolded text of the Bible story script.

Form two groups of kids. Instruct the first group to find Mark 1:21-28 in their Bibles. Instruct the second group to find Luke 4:31-37. Ask the following review questions. When a group finds the answer in its assigned passage, the kids in the group should stand. Each answer is found in both Gospels. Call on someone from each group to read the verse that reveals the answer.

Point out that Mark and Luke wrote about the same event, but their stories are not exactly the same because they each wrote from a different perspective. What Mark saw or heard about the event might not be exactly the same as what Luke saw or heard about it.

1. Jesus and His disciples were in what city?
   (*Capernaum; Mark 1:21; Luke 4:31*)

2. On what day did Jesus go to the synagogue? (*on the Sabbath; Mark 1:21; Luke 4:31*)

3. Why were the people amazed at Jesus' teaching? (*He taught as one having authority; Mark 1:22; Luke 4:32*)

4. What was wrong with the man in the synagogue? (*He had an evil [unclean] spirit inside him; Mark 1:23; Luke 4:33*)

5. What did Jesus say to the evil spirit? (*"Be quiet and come out of him!" Mark 1:25; Luke 4:35*)

6. What did Jesus show His power over? (*evil [unclean] spirits; Mark 1:27; Luke 4:36*)

Say • Good work, everyone! The Gospels of Mark and Luke both tell us about Jesus driving out an unclean spirit. Say the big picture question and answer with me. ***What did the evil spirit know about Jesus? Jesus is the Holy One of God.***

If you choose to review with boys and girls how to become a Christian, explain that kids are welcome to speak with you or another teacher if they have questions.

- **God rules.** God created and is in charge of everything. (Gen. 1:1; Rev. 4:11; Col. 1:16-17)
- **We sinned.** Since Adam and Eve, everyone has chosen to disobey God. (Rom. 3:23; 6:23)
- **God provided.** God sent His Son, Jesus, to rescue us from the punishment we deserve. (John 3:16; Eph. 2:8-9)
- **Jesus gives.** Jesus lived a perfect life, died on the cross for our sins, and rose again so we can be welcomed into God's family. (Rom. 5:8; 2 Cor. 5:21; 1 Pet. 3:18)
- **We respond.** Believe that Jesus alone saves you. Repent. Tell God that your faith is in Jesus. (Rom. 10:9-10,13)

Activity choice (10 minutes)

Option 1: Who has the crown?

- paper
- scissors
- tape
- music
- "This Is Amazing Grace" song (optional)

Create a simple paper crown. Instruct kids to stand shoulder-to-shoulder in a circle and put their hands behind their backs. Choose a volunteer to stand in the middle of the circle and cover his eyes. Give one kid the paper crown. Explain that at your signal, kids should pass the crown around the circle behind their backs.

Say "go" or start the music to signal kids to begin. After a few moments, pause the music or say "stop." The kid in the middle should uncover his eyes. Give the volunteer one to three chances to guess who has the crown.

If the player at the center guesses who has the crown, he should trade places with that player and kids can play again. If he does not guess who has the crown, assign another volunteer to be in the center.

Say • Jesus has authority over evil. He has authority over all things because He is King, and He came to make all things right. One day Jesus will take away Satan, sin, and death once and for all.

• *What did the evil spirit know about Jesus? Jesus is the Holy One of God.*

Option 2: Air power demonstration

• balloons
• masking tape
• fishing line, 25 feet
• plastic drinking straw
• chairs, 2

Choose four volunteers to assist you. Position two chairs facing away from each other approximately 20 feet apart. Instruct two kids to sit in the chairs to keep them from tipping over. Slip a plastic drinking straw onto the fishing line and tape the line between the two chairs.

Give the third kid a balloon. Ask him to inflate it and pinch it closed. Give the fourth kid a piece of masking tape to carefully tape the balloon to the drinking straw. Position the straw at one end of the fishing line. Signal the third kid to let go of the balloon. The force of the air escaping from the balloon should propel the straw down the fishing line.

As time allows, reset the demonstration and allow other kids to participate. Provide a new balloon for each kid.

Say • We could see the power of the air coming out of the balloon because it moved the straw. When Jesus drove out the evil spirit in today's Bible story, He showed that He has power over all our enemies.

• *What did the evil spirit know about Jesus? Jesus is the Holy One of God.*

Journal and prayer (5 minutes)

• pencils
• journals
• Bibles
• Journal Page, 1 per kid (enhanced CD)
• "I Know Who You Are" activity page, 1 per kid

Say • Draw or write something you know is true about Jesus. Think about the Bible story, the big picture question, and the key passage.

Invite kids to share prayer requests. Close the group in prayer. As time allows, lead kids to complete the activity page "I Know Who You Are."

Leader BIBLE STUDY

Jesus' fame was increasing. His ministry had begun with the calling of His disciples. Now Jesus traveled with them in the region of Galilee, teaching and performing miracles. The people recognized that Jesus wasn't like other teachers; He taught with authority. He had even demonstrated His power over unclean spirits by healing a man in the synagogue. News about Jesus was spreading. The subject of conversation around Galilee was changing. Who was this Jesus?

3 Jesus was in Capernaum when He went into the house of Simon Peter and Andrew, two of His disciples. Peter's mother-in-law also lived in the house, but she was ill. A fever had confined her to bed. Jesus' disciples told Jesus about the woman's condition, and Jesus went to her side. Touching the woman's hand, Jesus healed her. She immediately got up and began to serve Jesus and the others in the house. Serving Jesus and living for Him is how we can show we are thankful to Him.

People in the area heard about the healing of Peter's mother-in-law, and they came to Jesus to be healed too. That evening, people came to Jesus afflicted by illness or unclean spirits, and Jesus healed them.

The Gospel of Matthew says that in doing this, Jesus fulfilled the prophecy of Isaiah: "He Himself took our weaknesses and carried our diseases" (Isa. 53:5). Isaiah described the promised Messiah as a suffering servant who would suffer—not for His sins, but for our sins. He would die the death we deserve to free us from sin and death.

Illness is an effect of man's sinful rebellion against God. God never intended for people to be crippled by the numerous physical ailments in this world. Jesus offered physical healings to the crowd, and He can heal us in this life or in the life to come. Jesus' healings brought a glimpse into the kingdom of God, the world in which Jesus makes all things new—the way God intended—when He comes again. (See Rev. 21:4-5.)

Older Kids BIBLE STUDY OVERVIEW

Session Title: Jesus Healed Peter's Mother-in-Law
Bible Passage: Matthew 8:14-17; Mark 1:29-31; Luke 4:38-39
Big Picture Question: How can we show we are thankful to Jesus? We
   can serve Jesus and live for Him.
Key Passage: John 20:30-31
Unit Christ Connection: Jesus' miracles demonstrated His divine
   authority.

3

Small Group Opening

Large Group Leader

Small Group Leader

THE BIBLE STORY

Jesus Healed Peter's Mother-in-Law
Matthew 8:14-17; Mark 1:29-31; Luke 4:38-39

Jesus was at Capernaum (kuh PUHR nay uhm) **in Galilee** (GAL ih lee). **It was the Sabbath day, and Jesus had been teaching people in the synagogue about God.** While He was in the synagogue, He had commanded an evil spirit to leave a man. And the spirit had obeyed Jesus' command!

People all over the region were talking about Jesus. They were telling others about the things Jesus taught, the way He taught with authority, and about the miraculous ways He had helped people. No one had ever met anyone like Him before.

After Jesus left the synagogue, He went right away to the home of Peter and his brother Andrew. Peter lived there with his wife and his wife's mother. **Peter's mother-in-law was lying in bed. She was sick—suffering from a high fever. The people in the house told Jesus about her, so Jesus went to see her.**

Jesus touched her hand, and the fever left her right away. Jesus helped Peter's mother-in-law stand up. She didn't feel just a little better; she was completely better! She wasn't sick anymore because Jesus had healed her! **Right away, the woman began to serve Jesus and the others there.**

That evening, people brought to Jesus their friends and family members, anyone who needed help. So many people came; it looked as if the whole town was standing outside the door, waiting to see Jesus. These people were sick; some of them had evil spirits. **The people had heard about Jesus and how He had healed people and drove out evil spirits. They hoped Jesus would help them too.**

Jesus did help the people who came to Him. He spoke a word to make the evil spirits go away. He put His hands on the people who were sick, and He healed them. Jesus did these things so that the words of Isaiah the prophet would come true. In the Old Testament, Isaiah had written about Jesus: "He Himself took our weaknesses and carried our diseases."

Christ Connection: The prophet Isaiah wrote that the promised Messiah would bear our sickness and carry our pain. Jesus fulfilled this prophecy as He healed people. Sickness exists because the world is broken by sin. One day, when Jesus returns, there will be no more sickness because Jesus dealt with sin on the cross.

Small Group OPENING

Session Title: Jesus Healed Peter's Mother-in-Law
Bible Passage: Matthew 8:14-17; Mark 1:29-31; Luke 4:38-39
Big Picture Question: How can we show we are thankful to Jesus? We can serve Jesus and live for Him.
Key Passage: John 20:30-31
Unit Christ Connection: Jesus' miracles demonstrated His divine authority.

Welcome time

Greet each kid as he or she arrives. Use this time to collect the offering, fill out attendance sheets, and help new kids connect to your group.

Encourage kids to think about a time someone they know was sick. Did they visit that person? Did they do anything for that person?

Activity page (5 minutes)

- *"Danke!* Thanks!" activity page, 1 per kid
- pencils

Invite kids to work individually or in pairs to complete the activity page "*Danke*! Thanks!" Kids will try to match each language with its translation of the English phrase *thank you*. Use the pronunciation guide to help kids pronounce each word.

After a couple of minutes, ask the kids to share their answers. Gently correct any misinterpretations. (*Swahili:* asante; *French:* merci; *German:* danke; *Hawaiian:* mahalo; *Italian,* grazie; *Japanese:* arigato; *Spanish:* gracias)

Say • We can say thank you when someone does something kind for us. In today's Bible story, Jesus helped a woman, and the woman showed she was thankful.

Session starter (10 minutes)

Option 1: Who's who?

Write the following family roles on separate index cards: *husband*, *wife*, *mother*, *father*, *mother-in-law*, *father-in-law*, *son*, *daughter*. Distribute them to eight volunteers. Instruct the volunteers to stand before the group and hold up their cards. Name the husband *Aaron* and the wife *Maya*.

Read the following descriptions and challenge the class to identify how that family member is related to Aaron.

- The woman Aaron married (*Aaron's wife, Maya*)
- The grandson of Aaron's mother (*Aaron's son*)
- The father of Aaron's wife (*Aaron's father-in-law*)
- The mother of Aaron's wife (*Aaron's mother-in-law*)

Say • Today we are going to hear from the Bible about a time Jesus helped His disciple's mother-in-law.

Option 2: Problem/solution pairs

Print and cut apart the problem/solution cards. Distribute the cards to kids. If your group is large, copy the blank cards to prepare more sets.

Explain that half of the kids' cards explain a problem while the other half of the cards offer a solution. Challenge kids to match the problems and solutions. When kids make a match, that pair should sit down.

When all the kids are seated, call on each pair to share its problem and solution. Invite kids to suggest other possible solutions for the problem. Applaud kids for their creativity and problem-solving skills.

Say • In today's Bible story, someone was sick and needed help. Only one person could heal her. We'll find out who soon.

Transition to large group

materials (left margin):
- index cards
- marker

- "Problem/Solution Cards" (enhanced CD)
- scissors

Large Group LEADER

Session Title: Jesus Healed Peter's Mother-in-Law
Bible Passage: Matthew 8:14-17; Mark 1:29-31; Luke 4:38-39
Big Picture Question: How can we show we are thankful to Jesus? We can serve Jesus and live for Him.
Key Passage: John 20:30-31
Unit Christ Connection: Jesus' miracles demonstrated His divine authority.

Countdown

• countdown video

Show the countdown video as your kids arrive, and set it to end as large group time begins.

Introduce the session (2 minutes)

• leader attire
• football

[Large Group Leader enters carrying a football and wearing football cleats and eye black or anti-glare face strips. Leader holds football as if ready to throw it.]

Leader • Go long! Go long! *[Pause and look disappointed when no one moves to catch the ball.]* Well, that's OK. We probably shouldn't play football indoors anyway. I'm glad you're here! I'm [*your name*] and—as you might have noticed—another week, another sport. I'm trying football this week. Practice is tomorrow. I can't decide what position I want to play. I think I want to be a quarterback or a kicker. What do you think?

Well, it's time to get started. Are you ready for today's Bible story? I wonder what we will learn about today. We better look at the timeline map.

Timeline map (2 minutes)

• Timeline Map

Use the timeline map to point out and review the previous

Bible stories, "Jesus Healed an Official's Son" and "Jesus Drove Out Evil Spirits." Invite kids to share any details they remember about the Bible stories.

Leader • Jesus performed many miracles while He was on earth. *What happened when Jesus performed miracles? Jesus' miracles helped people believe in Him.* The official and everyone in his household believed in Jesus when the sick boy was healed. Then Jesus commanded an evil spirit to go away, and the evil spirit obeyed Him. *What did the evil spirit know about Jesus? Jesus is the Holy One of God.*

Today, we're going to hear about another miracle Jesus did. Today's Bible story is called "Jesus Healed Peter's Mother-in-Law."

Big picture question (1 minute)

Leader • Wow. All these people Jesus healed must have been very thankful. That leads me to our big picture question. Our big picture question is, *How can we show we are thankful to Jesus?* Sometimes when I'm thankful to someone, I send a thank-you card. Let's listen to the Bible story to find out how we can thank Jesus.

Tell the Bible story (10 minutes)

• "Jesus Healed Peter's Mother-in-Law" video
• Bibles, 1 per kid
• Bible Story Picture Slide or Poster
• Big Picture Question Slide or Poster

Open your Bible to Matthew 8:14-17; Mark 1:29-31; or Luke 4:38-39. Tell the Bible story in your own words, or show the Bible story video "Jesus Healed Peter's Mother-in-Law."

Leader • Peter and his brother Andrew lived in a house in Capernaum (kuh PUHR nay uhm). Peter's wife lived there too, and his mother-in-law—his wife's mother— lived with them. Jesus came to the house, and the people there told Jesus that Peter's mother-in-law was sick. She had a high fever and was lying in bed.

Do you think the people in the house knew Jesus could heal Peter's mother-in-law? They had probably heard stories of Jesus healing other people. So Jesus went to see Peter's mother-in-law. He went to her bedside and touched her hand. Guess what! Her fever left right away. It wasn't that she had less of a fever; she had no fever at all! Jesus healed her completely! That is a miracle!

Jesus helped Peter's mother-in-law stand up, and she began to serve Jesus and the other people in the house. The woman was so thankful. You know, I think that is our big picture question. ***How can we show we are thankful to Jesus? We can serve Jesus and live for Him.***

That's what Peter's mother-in-law did. Say the big picture question and answer with me. ***How can we show we are thankful to Jesus? We can serve Jesus and live for Him.***

You can probably imagine that word spread quickly about what Jesus had done. That evening, lots of people came to the house to see Jesus. They brought their friends and family members who were sick or hurting, and Jesus healed them too.

Did you know that hundreds of years before Jesus was born on earth, the prophet Isaiah wrote that Jesus would do these things? In the Old Testament, Isaiah wrote that Jesus would take our sickness and carry our pain.

Jesus healed people physically, but He also died on the cross to heal people spiritually. You see, everyone sins. Think about sin like a sickness. Because God is holy, He cannot be around sin. Jesus died on the cross to take the punishment we deserve for our sins. When we trust in Jesus, He takes away our sin, and we can live with God forever in heaven. That's good news.

The Gospel: God's Plan for Me (optional)

• Bible

Using Scripture and the guide provided, explain to boys and girls how to become a Christian. Tell kids how they can respond, and provide counselors to speak with each kid individually. Guide counselors to use open-ended questions to allow kids to determine the direction of the conversation.

Encourage boys and girls to ask their parents, small group leaders, or other adults any questions they may have about becoming a Christian.

Key passage (5 minutes)

• Key Passage Slide or Poster
• "Written" song

Leader • I love reading about Jesus' miracles. Each of these stories is in the Bible for a reason. Do you remember what that reason is? Can anyone say our key passage from memory?

Invite any kids who know John 20:30-31 to recite it aloud. Then lead kids to find John 20:30-31 in their Bibles. Lead the class to read the verses aloud together.

Leader • These verses tell us why the apostle John wrote about Jesus' miracles in his Gospel. And these aren't even all of the miraculous signs Jesus performed! But the Book of John contains these stories so that we can read them and believe that Jesus is the Messiah, the Son of God. And when we believe that, we have eternal life. Let's sing our key passage song together.

Sing "Written."

Discussion starter video (5 minutes)

• "Unit 26 Session 3" discussion starter video

Leader • Has someone ever done something nice for you? Did you do or say anything to thank that person? Let's watch this video.

Show the "Unit 26 Session 3" video.

Leader • How do you think you should react when another

person helps you? Should you complain? What are some ways you can show you are thankful? *How can we show we are thankful to Jesus? We can serve Jesus and live for Him.*

• "This Is Amazing Grace" song

Sing (3 minutes)

Leader • One way we can show Jesus that we are thankful to Him is by praising Him. Let's sing together.

Choose one or two volunteers to lead kids in singing "This Is Amazing Grace."

Prayer (2 minutes)

Leader • That was wonderful. Thanks, everyone. I'm so glad you could come. Will you be back next week? I can't wait to hear another story about Jesus' miracles. Before you go to your small groups, I'm going to pray.

Close the group in prayer. Thank God for sending Jesus to earth to rescue people from sins. Thank Him for Jesus' miracles which help people believe that He is the Messiah, the Son of God. Ask Him to heal those who are sick or hurting, and ask Him to help us trust that Jesus will return one day and take away sin and sickness forever.

Dismiss to small groups

The Gospel: God's Plan for Me

Ask kids if they have ever heard the word *gospel*. Clarify that the word *gospel* means "good news." It is the message about Christ, the kingdom of God, and salvation. Use the following guide to share the gospel with kids.

God rules. Explain to kids that the Bible tells us God created everything, and He is in charge of everything. Invite a volunteer to read Genesis 1:1 from the Bible. Read Revelation 4:11 or Colossians 1:16-17 aloud and explain what these verses mean.

We sinned. Tell kids that since the time of Adam and Eve, everyone has chosen to disobey God. (Romans 3:23) The Bible calls this sin. Because God is holy, God cannot be around sin. Sin separates us from God and deserves God's punishment of death. (Romans 6:23)

God provided. Choose a child to read John 3:16 aloud. Say that God sent His Son, Jesus, the perfect solution to our sin problem, to rescue us from the punishment we deserve. It's something we, as sinners, could never earn on our own. Jesus alone saves us. Read and explain Ephesians 2:8-9.

Jesus gives. Share with kids that Jesus lived a perfect life, died on the cross for our sins, and rose again. Because Jesus gave up His life for us, we can be welcomed into God's family for eternity. This is the best gift ever! Read Romans 5:8; 2 Corinthians 5:21; or 1 Peter 3:18.

We respond. Tell kids that they can respond to Jesus. Read Romans 10:9-10,13. Review these aspects of our response: Believe in your heart that Jesus alone saves you through what He's already done on the cross. Repent, turning from self and sin to Jesus. Tell God and others that your faith is in Jesus.

Offer to talk with any child who is interested in responding to Jesus.

Small Group LEADER

Session Title: Jesus Healed Peter's Mother-in-Law
Bible Passage: Matthew 8:14-17; Mark 1:29-31; Luke 4:38-39
Big Picture Question: How can we show we are thankful to Jesus? We can serve Jesus and live for Him.
Key Passage: John 20:30-31
Unit Christ Connection: Jesus' miracles demonstrated His divine authority.

Key passage activity (5 minutes)

• Key Passage Poster
• poster board
• sticky notes
• marker

Write the key passage on a piece of poster board, drawing blanks for several of the words. Write the missing words on separate sticky notes and hide them around the room.

Show the key passage poster and lead kids to recite the verse once or twice. Then cover the poster and display the poster board with blanks. Challenge kids to search around the room for the missing words. When kids find the missing words, they should stick them to the poster board in the appropriate spaces. Applaud kids for their work and allow kids to take turns saying the passage from memory.

Say • Nice work! The Book of John contains these stories about Jesus' miracles so that we will believe that Jesus is the Messiah, the Son of God.

Bible story review & Bible skills (10 minutes)

• Bibles, 1 per kid
• Small Group Visual Pack

Review the timeline in the small group visual pack. Retell or review the Bible story in your own words or use the bolded text of the Bible story script. Point out that today's Bible story is found in three of the four Gospels: Matthew, Mark, and Luke. Ask kids to describe what the Gospels are about. (*Jesus' life, death, and resurrection*)

Invite kids to spread out around the room and lie on their backs. Explain that you will ask a question about the Bible story. If a kid knows the answer, she should stand up. Call on someone who is standing to answer the review question. If she is correct, instruct her to remain standing. Direct the remaining kids to lie back down. Then ask another question.

1. Which disciple's house did Jesus go to? (*Peter's house; Matt. 8:14; Mark 1:29; Luke 4:38*)
2. Which of Peter's relatives was lying in bed? (*Peter's mother-in-law; Matt. 8:14; Mark 1:30; Luke 4:38*)
3. What was wrong with Peter's mother-in-law? (*She was sick and had a fever; Matt. 8:14; Mark 1:30; Luke 4:38*)
4. What did Jesus do to heal Peter's mother-in-law? (*He touched her hand; Matt. 8:15; Mark 1:31*)
5. What did Peter's mother-in-law do after Jesus healed her? (*She got up and began to serve Him; Matt. 8:15; Mark 1:31; Luke 4:39*)
6. Who came to Jesus to be healed? (*people who were sick or who had evil spirits, Matt. 8:16*)
7. What did Jesus do to help the people who came to Him? (*He drove out the evil spirits and healed those who were sick, Matt. 8:16*)
8. What Scripture did Jesus fulfill? (*the words of the prophet Isaiah, Matt. 8:17*)
9. ***How can we show we are thankful to Jesus? We can serve Jesus and live for Him.***

If you choose to review with boys and girls how to become a Christian, explain that kids are welcome to speak with you or another teacher if they have questions.

- **God rules.** God created and is in charge of everything. (Gen. 1:1; Rev. 4:11; Col. 1:16-17)
- **We sinned.** Since Adam and Eve, everyone has

chosen to disobey God. (Rom. 3:23; 6:23)

- **God provided.** God sent His Son, Jesus, to rescue us from the punishment we deserve. (John 3:16; Eph. 2:8-9)
- **Jesus gives.** Jesus lived a perfect life, died on the cross for our sins, and rose again so we can be welcomed into God's family. (Rom. 5:8; 2 Cor. 5:21; 1 Pet. 3:18)
- **We respond.** Believe that Jesus alone saves you. Repent. Tell God that your faith is in Jesus. (Rom. 10:9-10,13)

- paper
- markers
- stickers or other decorating supplies (optional)

Activity choice (10 minutes)

Option 1: Get-well-soon cards

Provide paper and markers for kids to make get-well-soon cards for kids or adults who are sick. You may choose to provide stickers or other decorating supplies for kids to use.

Invite kids to write encouraging messages in the cards and suggest they write Isaiah's words from Matthew 8:17.

Arrange to mail or deliver the cards to people in your church or community who are sick.

Say • Sometimes people who are sick can feel discouraged. We can let them know that we are praying for them. We can show them the love of Jesus by serving them. *How can we show we are thankful to Jesus? We can serve Jesus and live for Him*. Let's pray.

- Lord, You have the power to heal people who are sick or hurting. We pray that You would. But even if You don't, please help us to trust that You are good. We know that one day Jesus will come back and take away sin and suffering forever. Come, Lord Jesus. We love You. Amen.

Option 2: Silly supper service

Guide kids to sit around a table. Give each kid a sticky note and pencil. Instruct each kid to write his name on the sticky note. Read the following menu options. Each kid should choose an option and write it on his sticky note. Do not reveal to kids what each option represents.

1. Harvest helpings
2. Briny branches
3. Tasteful tidbits

Choose three kids to be servers. Servers will collect and sort the sticky notes. Prepare the snacks to be served in paper cups. Allow the servers to give each kid the snack he ordered. ("Harvest helpings" are fruit slices, "briny branches" are pretzel sticks, and "tasteful tidbits" are candy-coated chocolate pieces)

Be aware of any food allergies kids may have. If you wish, serve the other snacks as well if kids are not happy with the selections they made.

Say • Were you surprised at the snack you were served? Let's thank our servers for bringing us these tasty snacks. [*Lead kids to clap or say thank you.*]

• *How can we show we are thankful to Jesus? We can serve Jesus and live for Him.*

Journal and prayer (5 minutes)

Say • Write in your journal about a time you were thankful. How did you show it? List some ways you can show thanks to Jesus.

Invite kids to share prayer requests. Close the group in prayer, or allow a couple volunteers to close the group in prayer. As time allows, lead kids to complete the activity page "Jesus Healed Crossword."

Sidebar materials:
- fruit slices
- pretzel sticks
- candy-coated chocolate pieces
- paper cups
- sticky notes
- pencils
- Allergy Alert (enhanced CD)

- pencils
- journals
- Bibles
- Journal Page, 1 per kid (enhanced CD)
- "Jesus Healed Crossword" activity page, 1 per kid

Leader BIBLE STUDY

In ancient Israel, living with a skin disease wasn't easy. It was painful and isolating. Leprosy is a disease caused by bacteria, and it affects the skin, nerves, and mucous membranes. The disease can cause deformities in hands and feet and paralysis of some muscles. Leprosy is contagious, and the people of Israel had laws about what to do when a person becomes infected.

First, the person would go to a priest. The priest would examine him, and if the disease was confirmed, the priest would declare the person to be unclean. The law in Leviticus 13:45-46 says that the infected person must tear his clothes and let his hair hang loose. He must cover his mouth and cry out, "Unclean, unclean!" This was a warning for others to stay away from him. The infected person must live alone outside the camp.

When the person's disease was healed, he had to be declared "clean" by the priest. This involved an examination and the sacrifice of animals. The person had to wash his clothes, shave his hair, and take a bath. Then he had to wait outside the camp for a week and wash again. The priest would make an atonement for the person who was cleansed. (See Lev. 14:1-32.)

A man with a serious skin disease approached Jesus and fell down before Him. "If You are willing, You can make me clean," he said. The man's words were more of a truthful declaration than a request. He clearly trusted in Jesus' power to heal people, and he longed to be healed himself.

Jesus reached out and touched the man. "I am willing," He said. Typically, no one touched a leper. Touching an unclean person would make you unclean too. But Jesus didn't become unclean. Instead, the diseased man was immediately healed.

As you teach kids the story of Jesus cleansing a leper, help them consider how sin affects all of us. Like leprosy, its effects are painful. Sin separates us from God. Jesus willingly died on the cross and rose from the dead to rescue us from sin and gives us new life.

Older Kids BIBLE STUDY OVERVIEW

Session Title: Jesus Cleansed a Leper

Bible Passage: Matthew 8:1-4; Mark 1:40-45; Luke 5:12-16

Big Picture Question: Who can take away our sin? Jesus can and wants to cleanse us from sin.

Key Passage: John 20:30-31

Unit Christ Connection: Jesus' miracles demonstrated His divine authority.

Small Group Opening

Large Group Leader

Small Group Leader

The BIBLE STORY

Jesus Cleansed a Leper
Matthew 8:1-4; Mark 1:40-45; Luke 5:12-16

Jesus had been healing people in Galilee and teaching in the synagogue. **One morning, Jesus got up early and went up on a mountain to pray. When He came down from the mountain, large crowds of people had gathered together, and they followed Jesus.**

Jesus came to a town where a man lived who had leprosy, a serious skin disease. God's people had laws about how to deal with people who had a skin disease. These people were considered "unclean." **A person with a skin disease had to live alone, away from everyone else. He had to tear his clothes, cover his mouth, and say, "Unclean! Unclean!" because if he touched anyone else, that person would become unclean too.**

When the man with the skin disease saw Jesus, he fell facedown before Him. The man begged Jesus to heal him. "If You are willing, Lord, You can make me clean," he said.

Jesus reached out His hand and touched the man. What was Jesus doing? Didn't He know that touching an unclean person could make Him unclean too? But **Jesus said, "I am willing. Be made clean."**

Instead of the man making Jesus unclean, Jesus' touch made the man clean. **The man's skin disease was immediately gone. He was healed!**

Jesus ordered the man to keep quiet. "Don't tell anyone what you have seen. Go to the priest and show him that you are no longer unclean, and then make the sacrifice according to the law of Moses."

But the man did not keep quiet like Jesus asked him to do. Right away, he went out and told anyone who would listen that Jesus had healed him. News about Jesus spread throughout the area, and large crowds of people came to Jesus to hear Him teach and to be healed of their sicknesses.

Jesus could no longer walk into a town without being noticed. He often withdrew to deserted places so He could be alone to pray, but even there people found Him, and they came from every direction to see Him.

Christ Connection: Not only did Jesus have the power to make a leper clean, He was willing to make him clean. Like the disease of leprosy, sin deeply affects all people and makes them spiritually dead. Jesus willingly died on the cross and rose from the dead to save us from our sin and give us new life.

Small Group OPENING

Session Title: Jesus Cleansed a Leper
Bible Passage: Matthew 8:1-4; Mark 1:40-45; Luke 5:12-16
Big Picture Question: Who can take away our sin? Jesus can and wants to cleanse us from sin.
Key Passage: John 20:30-31
Unit Christ Connection: Jesus' miracles demonstrated His divine authority.

Welcome time

Greet each kid as he or she arrives. Use this time to collect the offering, fill out attendance sheets, and help new kids connect to your group. Ask kids to describe how they feel when they are alone. Discuss what kids do when they feel lonely.

Activity page (5 minutes)

- "Get Well Soon" activity page, 1 per kid
- pencils

Invite kids to work in small groups to complete the activity page "Get Well Soon." Kids should underline the things a person with a skin disease had to do in ancient Israel. They should circle the things a sick person might do today.

Provide Bibles and guide kids to find and read Leviticus 13:1-3,45-46 if they need help figuring out what to underline. (*Be examined by a priest; tear your clothes; let your hair hang loose; live alone away from others; cover your mouth and cry out, "Unclean, unclean!"*)

Say • People in ancient Israel did some strange things when they were sick. Today we are going to hear a story about a man in ancient Israel who had a skin disease. The man went to Jesus for help. Do you think Jesus helped him?

Session starter (10 minutes)

Option 1: Perfect circle challenge

Give each child a marker and a piece of paper. Challenge each kid to draw a perfect circle. A perfect circle is completely round. Encourage kids to make their best attempts. When kids finish, tape their papers to a focal wall where everyone can see them or spread them out on a table or open area on the floor. Allow kids to decide whose circle is the closest to being perfect.

Say • All of you tried hard, and the circle you chose as the best is pretty good, but it's not perfect. Today's Bible story will remind us of the only One who is perfect.

- paper
- markers
- tape (optional)

Option 2: Clean it up

Clear a large area for kids to play an active game. Use tape to mark a large square or circle on the floor. Put a large number of balloons or paper wads inside the circle.

Form two even teams. Instruct one team to stand inside the circle and the other team to stand outside the circle. Explain that at your signal, the kids inside the circle should begin moving the paper wads outside the circle. The kids outside the circle should try to move the paper wads back inside the circle. After a couple of minutes, call teams to stop. See which area is more clear of paper wads.

Now, give new rules. Kids outside the circle may only move the paper wads using their feet. Signal for kids to begin. If kids are able to clear the circle of all the paper wads, call kids to stop.

- balloons or paper wads
- masking tape or painter's tape

Say • Today we are going to hear a story from the Bible about a man who had a skin disease. He asked Jesus to make Him clean, and that's exactly what Jesus did.

Transition to large group

Large Group LEADER

Session Title: Jesus Cleansed a Leper
Bible Passage: Matthew 8:1-4; Mark 1:40-45; Luke 5:12-16
Big Picture Question: Who can take away our sin? Jesus can and wants to cleanse us from sin.
Key Passage: John 20:30-31
Unit Christ Connection: Jesus' miracles demonstrated His divine authority.

Countdown

• countdown video

Show the countdown video as your kids arrive, and set it to end as large group time begins.

Introduce the session (2 minutes)

• leader attire
• basketball

[Large Group Leader enters wearing sweatbands and basketball shoes. Leader dribbles a basketball a couple of times and then picks it up.]

Leader • Hey, everyone! I'm glad you're back! In case you're new here, I'm [*your name*]. As you can tell, I'm trying out for a basketball team. Baseball didn't work out, bowling was a bust, and football wasn't my thing. But I have a great feeling about basketball. Do any of you know how to play basketball? You will have to give me a few pointers later. For now, let's get ready to hear today's Bible story. Who remembers what Bible stories we've studied so far? Let's check out our timeline map to review where we've been in God's big story.

Timeline map (2 minutes)

• Timeline Map

Use the timeline map to point out and review the previous Bible stories: "Jesus Healed an Official's Son," "Jesus

Drove Out Evil Spirits," and "Jesus Healed Peter's Mother-in-Law."

Leader • Look at our timeline map. These last few stories have been all about Jesus' miracles. These are so amazing. Who else can heal a sick boy from miles away, or command an evil spirit to go away, or touch a woman's hand and heal her from her fever? Only Jesus can!

Jesus is the Holy One of God, and when He performed miracles, people believed in Him. Today we are going to hear about another miracle. This Bible story is called "Jesus Cleansed a Leper."

Big picture question (1 minute)

Leader • Hmm …do you know what a leper is? A *leper* is someone who has leprosy. Now you might be wondering, *What's leprosy?* Well, leprosy is a serious skin disease. You'll see in the Bible story that this serious skin disease reminds us of sin. That leads me to our big picture question. Our big picture question is, **Who can take away our sin?** Now, you may think you already know the answer. Listen carefully to the Bible story to see if you are right.

Tell the Bible story (10 minutes)

• "Jesus Cleansed a Leper" video
• Bibles
• Bible Story Picture Slide or Poster
• Big Picture Question Slide or Poster

Open your Bible to Matthew 8:1-4; Mark 1:40-45; or Luke 5:12-16. Tell the Bible story in your own words or show the Bible story video "Jesus Cleansed a Leper."

Leader • Jesus traveled a lot during His ministry. One day, He came to a town where a man lived. This man had a serious skin disease called leprosy. Leprosy affected everything about this man's life. He couldn't hang out with his friends or go to the synagogue or hug his parents. He had to live by himself, far away from everyone else.

He was probably very lonely.

God's people had laws about what to do when a person had leprosy. This man had to tear his clothes and cover his mouth. He had to say, "Unclean! Unclean!" to warn others that he was sick. If he got too close to someone else, that person would be called unclean too.

Oh, how I bet that man wished he were better! On that day, he saw Jesus. Surely he heard of the miracles Jesus had done and how Jesus had healed other people. So the man fell down in front of Jesus. What did he say to Jesus? He said, "If You are willing, Lord, You can make me clean." That wasn't even a question! The man was saying what he knew was true. If Jesus wanted to heal the man, He could.

Do you think Jesus said, "Get away from Me! You're unclean!"? No! Of course not. Jesus said, "I am willing. Be made clean." Then Jesus touched the man and the man's skin disease was gone! He was healed!

What a happy day! The healed man probably wanted to go tell everyone he saw that he was all better and that Jesus had healed him. But Jesus told the man to keep quiet and to go to the priest. But the man didn't keep quiet. He told everyone what happened, and news about Jesus spread. Many people came to be healed and to hear Jesus teach.

Now, you've probably never had leprosy, but we are all affected by something that we need to be healed from. Do you know what that is? It's sin. The Bible says that everyone has sinned, or disobeyed God. Sin is like leprosy because it keeps us away from God and it hurts us. The bad news is that we cannot do anything to heal ourselves from sin. But the good news is that there is someone who can!

Who can take away our sin? Jesus can and wants to

Older Kids Bible Study Leader Guide
Unit 26 • Session 4

cleanse us from sin. That's our big picture question and answer. Say it with me. ***Who can take away our sin? Jesus can and wants to cleanse us from sin.***

Jesus came into the world to rescue people from sin. He lived a perfect life and took the punishment we deserve for our sin when He died on the cross. Jesus was raised from the dead, and He is alive. When we trust in Jesus as Lord and Savior, God forgives our sins and gives us eternal life. We will live with Him forever in heaven.

The Gospel: God's Plan for Me (optional)

• Bible

Using Scripture and the guide provided, explain to boys and girls how to become a Christian. Tell kids how they can respond, and provide counselors to speak with each kid individually. Encourage boys and girls to ask their parents, small group leaders, or other adults any questions they may have about becoming a Christian.

Key passage (5 minutes)

• Key Passage Slide or Poster
• "Written" song

Leader • Open your Bibles to John 20:30-31. Does anyone want to say our key passage from memory?
Invite volunteers to say the key passage aloud.
Leader • Can you tell me who wrote the Gospel of John? (*the apostle John*) John was one of Jesus' followers, and he wrote about many of the miracles Jesus did. He also wrote why these stories are in the Bible. Let's read the key passage together.
Lead boys and girls to read the key passage together. Then invite them to join in singing "Written."

Discussion starter video (5 minutes)

• "Unit 26 Session 4" discussion starter video

Leader • How many of you like helping others? Are there ever times you don't want to help someone else? What if you needed help and no one wanted to help you? Think about that as we watch this video.

Show the "Unit 26 Session 4" video.

Leader • Would you help a friend if he had a spider on him? Would you want someone to help you if a spider landed on you? I know I would. When Jesus healed the man who had leprosy, He didn't say, "OK, I guess I will help you if I have to." Jesus was willing! He *wanted* to help the man get better!

We need help because we do anything to get rid of sin on our own. **Who can take away our sin? Jesus can and wants to cleanse us from sin.** We can trust Him as Lord and Savior.

Sing (3 minutes)

• "This Is Amazing Grace" song

Leader • I am so glad that Jesus can and wants to take away our sin! That makes me want to sing. Will you praise Him with me?

Lead kids to sing "This Is Amazing Grace."

Prayer (2 minutes)

Leader • *Who can take away our sin? Jesus can and wants to cleanse us from sin.* Before you go to your small groups, let's pray.

Lord God, thank You for Your Son, Jesus. We confess that we have sinned. We trust that Jesus took our punishment instead. Please forgive us. Thank You for loving us and rescuing us from our sins. Amen.

Dismiss to small groups

The Gospel: God's Plan for Me

Ask kids if they have ever heard the word *gospel*. Clarify that the word *gospel* means "good news." It is the message about Christ, the kingdom of God, and salvation. Use the following guide to share the gospel with kids.

God rules. Explain to kids that the Bible tells us God created everything, and He is in charge of everything. Invite a volunteer to read Genesis 1:1 from the Bible. Read Revelation 4:11 or Colossians 1:16-17 aloud and explain what these verses mean.

We sinned. Tell kids that since the time of Adam and Eve, everyone has chosen to disobey God. (Romans 3:23) The Bible calls this sin. Because God is holy, God cannot be around sin. Sin separates us from God and deserves God's punishment of death. (Romans 6:23)

God provided. Choose a child to read John 3:16 aloud. Say that God sent His Son, Jesus, the perfect solution to our sin problem, to rescue us from the punishment we deserve. It's something we, as sinners, could never earn on our own. Jesus alone saves us. Read and explain Ephesians 2:8-9.

Jesus gives. Share with kids that Jesus lived a perfect life, died on the cross for our sins, and rose again. Because Jesus gave up His life for us, we can be welcomed into God's family for eternity. This is the best gift ever! Read Romans 5:8; 2 Corinthians 5:21; or 1 Peter 3:18.

We respond. Tell kids that they can respond to Jesus. Read Romans 10:9-10,13. Review these aspects of our response: Believe in your heart that Jesus alone saves you through what He's already done on the cross. Repent, turning from self and sin to Jesus. Tell God and others that your faith is in Jesus.

Offer to talk with any child who is interested in responding to Jesus.

Small Group LEADER

Session Title: Jesus Cleansed a Leper
Bible Passage: Matthew 8:1-4; Mark 1:40-45; Luke 5:12-16
Big Picture Question: Who can take away our sin? Jesus can and wants to cleanse us from sin.
Key Passage: John 20:30-31
Unit Christ Connection: Jesus' miracles demonstrated His divine authority.

Key passage activity (5 minutes)

- Key Passage Poster
- masking tape or painter's tape
- paper plates (optional)
- marker (optional)

Use tape to mark a large tic-tac-toe grid on the floor. Invite kids to play a game of human tic-tac-toe. Form two teams of five or more kids. If you have fewer than 10 kids, form two teams and give one team five paper plates marked with *X*s. Give the other team five paper plates marked with *O*s.

Choose one player to go first. Challenge the player to recite the key passage from memory. If she is successful, she may stand on or position a game piece on the tic-tac-toe board for her team. If she cannot recite the verse, play moves to the other team. Continue giving players a turn to recite the key passage. The first team to position three of its players or game pieces in a row wins. If the game ends in a draw, clear the gameboard and play again.

Say • Why are Jesus' miracles written in the Bible for us to read? These are written so that we may believe that Jesus is the Messiah, the Son of God.

Bible story review & Bible skills (10 minutes)

- Bibles, 1 per kid
- Small Group Visual Pack
- paper
- pens

Review the timeline in the small group visual pack. Form three groups of kids and assign each group one of the following passages: Matthew 8:1-4; Mark 1:40-45;

Luke 5:12-16. Instruct the kids in each group to read the passage together and draw a picture of a scene from the Bible story.

Give kids a few minutes to draw. Then invite them to share their drawings with the other groups. Ask kids the following review questions. If a group knows the answer, a player from that group should raise his hand. Call on a kid with his hand raised to answer. Note that some answers are found in just one or two of the Gospels.

1. Where was Jesus coming from when a man approached Him? (*the mountain, Matt. 8:1*)

2. What was wrong with the man? (*He had a serious skin disease; Matt. 8:2; Mark 1:40; Luke 5:12*)

3. What did the man ask Jesus to do? (*to make him clean; Matt. 8:2; Mark 1:40; Luke 5:12*)

4. How did Jesus heal the man? (*Jesus reached out His hand, touched the man, and said, "I am willing. Be made clean"; Matt. 8:3; Mark 1:41; Luke 5:13*)

5. Whom did Jesus instruct the man to tell about what happened? (*no one; Matt. 8:4; Mark 1:44; Luke 5:14*)

6. Where did Jesus tell the man to go? (*to the priest; Matt. 8:4; Mark 1:44; Luke 5:14*)

7. What did the man do when he left Jesus? (*He told everyone that Jesus had healed him; Mark 1:45*)

8. ***Who can take away our sin? Jesus can and wants to cleanse us from sin.***

If you choose to review with boys and girls how to become a Christian, explain that kids are welcome to speak with you or another teacher if they have questions.

- **God rules.** God created and is in charge of everything. (Gen. 1:1; Rev. 4:11; Col. 1:16-17)
- **We sinned.** Since Adam and Eve, everyone has

chosen to disobey God. (Rom. 3:23; 6:23)

- **God provided.** God sent His Son, Jesus, to rescue us from the punishment we deserve. (John 3:16; Eph. 2:8-9)
- **Jesus gives.** Jesus lived a perfect life, died on the cross for our sins, and rose again so we can be welcomed into God's family. (Rom. 5:8; 2 Cor. 5:21; 1 Pet. 3:18)
- **We respond.** Believe that Jesus alone saves you. Repent. Tell God that your faith is in Jesus. (Rom. 10:9-10,13)

• round red stickers

Activity choice (10 minutes)

Option 1: Reverse the curse

Give each kid two round red stickers. Instruct kids to put one sticker on each hand. Form two teams. Guide each team to sit together on the floor. Choose one player from each team to be the "doctor." Remove the doctors' stickers and invite the doctors to stand across the room from their teams. Explain that all the players are affected by a serious rash. The two doctors are the only ones who can heal them.

When you say go, each team must complete a relay. One player from each team will rush to the doctor, and the doctor will gently remove her "rash" (stickers). The healed player must return to her team, take a "sick" player by the hand, and lead him back to the doctor. When the doctor has healed the second player, the first and second player go together and lead another player to the doctor. Kids will continue leading players to the doctor one at a time until everyone on their team has been healed.

Say • We all sin. Sin is like a disease, and it separates us from God. ***Who can take away our sin? Jesus can and wants to cleanse us from sin.***

Option 2: Create the scene

Form four groups of kids. Give each group markers and a piece of poster board. Assign each group a passage from the Bible story:

- A man with leprosy came to Jesus. (Mark 1:40)
- Jesus healed the man with leprosy. (Mark 1:41-42)
- Jesus told the man what to do. (Mark 1:43-44)
- The man told everyone what happened. (Mark 1:45)

Guide each group to read its assigned passage in the Bible. Then instruct them to work together to draw the scene on their pieces of poster board.

Allow several minutes for groups to work. Then call on them to present their posters and retell the Bible story in order. Each group may read its assigned passage from the Bible, or kids may tell the story in their own words.

Say
- The man's disease separated him from everyone else, but Jesus healed him completely.
- Sin is like a disease that separates all of us from God. Jesus willingly died on the cross. He rose from the dead to save us from sin and give us new life.

Journal and prayer (5 minutes)

Give the following prompts and encourage kids to write their responses on the journal page.

Say
- What separates us from God? (*sin*)
- *Who can take away our sin? Jesus can and wants to cleanse us from sin.*
- Have you trusted in Jesus to take away your sin?

Be available to talk to any kids who have questions about becoming a Christian. Invite kids to share prayer requests. Close the group in prayer, or allow a couple volunteers to close the group in prayer. As time allows, lead kids to complete the activity page "Bible Truth Take Away."

Materials (margin column):
- poster board, 4 pieces
- markers
- Bibles

- pencils
- journals
- Bibles
- Journal Page, 1 per kid (enhanced CD)
- "Bible Truth Take Away" activity page, 1 per kid

Leader BIBLE STUDY

Jesus was in Capernaum, a city on the Sea of Galilee. The Pharisees and scribes—teachers of the law—came to listen to Jesus' teaching. They were curious about His message and wanted to make sure He was teaching things that were true. So many people came that they crowded the house; there was no more room.

That day, four friends came to see Jesus. The four men carried their friend who was paralyzed. Jesus had healed people before—even people who were paralyzed. (See Matt. 4:24; 8:6.) The men believed Jesus came from God, and He could heal people. So their faith led to action. Because the friends could not get through the crowd, they carried their friend to the roof and lowered him down to Jesus.

Jesus' words to the paralyzed man surprised the Pharisees and teachers of the law. Rather than saying, "Get up and walk," Jesus said, "Your sins are forgiven." The religious leaders kept quiet, but Jesus knew their thoughts. They accused Jesus of blasphemy, dishonoring God by claiming to do what only God can do. But Jesus did not blaspheme. He is God, and He has authority to forgive sins.

Jesus asked them, "Which is easier: to say, 'Your sins are forgiven,' or to say, 'Get up and walk'?" Simply saying, "Your sins are forgiven," seems to be the easier thing, but to actually forgive sins is harder, something only God can do. As God, Jesus has the power and authority to heal and forgive. And Jesus knew He would take the man's sins upon Himself on the cross—an act of love that would cost Him His life.

Jesus healed the paralyzed man to prove to the religious leaders His power to forgive. Mark 2:12 records the crowd's reaction: "They were all astounded and gave glory to God, saying, 'We have never seen anything like this!'"

Older Kids BIBLE STUDY OVERVIEW

Session Title: Four Friends Helped
Bible Passage: Matthew 9:1-8; Mark 2:1-12; Luke 5:17-26
Big Picture Question: How could Jesus forgive people's sins? Jesus was going to take the punishment for sin when He died on the cross.
Key Passage: John 20:30-31
Unit Christ Connection: Jesus' miracles demonstrated His divine authority.

Small Group Opening

Large Group Leader

Small Group Leader

The BIBLE STORY

Four Friends Helped
Matthew 9:1-8; Mark 2:1-12; Luke 5:17-26

Jesus had been traveling, and He went back to Capernaum (kuh PUHR nay uhm). **When the people in the town heard that Jesus was home, they gathered at the house to hear Him teach. Pharisees and other teachers of the law** had traveled from villages all over Galilee and Judea. Some even **came** from Jerusalem **to hear Jesus. So many people came that they stood in the doorway, and there was no more room for anyone else.**

Just then, four men came to the house. They were carrying their friend on a mat because he could not walk. They tried to bring their friend to Jesus because they wanted Jesus to heal him, **but they could not get through the crowd. So the men carried their friend up to the roof. They took off the roof above Jesus. Then they lowered their friend through the crowd** so that he was right in front of Jesus.

Jesus saw that the friends had faith, and He told the man lying on the mat, "Young man, your sins are forgiven!" When the religious leaders heard this, they thought, *Who does Jesus think He is? He is being disrespectful to God! Only God can forgive sins.*

Jesus knew what the religious leaders were thinking. He said to them, "Why are you thinking like that? **Is it easier for Me to say to this man, 'Your sins are forgiven,' or 'Get up and walk'?"**

As God's Son, Jesus had the power to forgive people's sins. But how could He prove that the man's sins were really forgiven? **So Jesus showed His power** on earth to forgive sins **by turning back to the man on the mat. "Get up, pick up your mat, and go home," Jesus said.**

The man who had been unable to walk **immediately got up. He picked up his mat, and he went home**, just like Jesus commanded.

Everyone in the crowd saw what happened, and they could hardly believe what they had seen! They **praised God and said, "We have never seen anything like this!"**

Christ Connection: The man who was paralyzed needed to be healed. Jesus knew this and did something even greater; Jesus forgave his sins, and then He healed the man. Because Jesus is God, He has the power and authority to heal and forgive. Jesus offers forgiveness to those who trust in Him.

Small Group OPENING

Session Title: Four Friends Helped
Bible Passage: Matthew 9:1-8; Mark 2:1-12; Luke 5:17-26
Big Picture Question: How could Jesus forgive people's sins? Jesus was going to take the punishment for sin when He died on the cross.
Key Passage: John 20:30-31
Unit Christ Connection: Jesus' miracles demonstrated His divine authority.

Welcome time

Greet each kid as he or she arrives. Use this time to collect the offering, fill out attendance sheets, and help new kids connect to your group.

Prompt each kid to think about one of his or her friends. What makes a good friend? Ask the kids if they would help a friend who needed help.

Activity page (5 minutes)

• "Four Friends" activity page, 1 per kid
• pencils

Invite kids to work individually or in pairs to complete the logic puzzle on the "Four Friends" activity page. Kids should read each clue to determine which friend attended which after-school activity and at what time. When kids solve the puzzle, they should use the letter clues below the blanks to determine what Jesus saw in four friends. (*faith*)

Say • Today's Bible story is about four friends who had faith. The friends believed that what Jesus said about Himself is true.

Session starter (10 minutes)

Option 1: Even better!

Guide kids to sit in a circle. Prompt the first kid to begin by saying, "I'd like to [*verb*], but [*verb*] would be even better!" For example, "I'd like to eat toast for breakfast, but bacon would be even better!"

Guide kids to take turns making their own "even better" statements. If kids struggle to come up with actions, suggest the primary action and allow them to state something that is even better. Consider the following suggestions: *go to the park, play basketball, watch a movie, eat a turkey sandwich, travel to New York City.*

Say • Our Bible story today is about four men who carried their friend to Jesus. The man couldn't walk and the friends believed Jesus could heal him. What Jesus did for him was even better!

Option 2: Four friends help

Create an indoor obstacle course by using tape to mark a path through the room. Use chairs or classroom furniture as obstacles for kids to go around, under, or over.

Form groups of four kids. Give each group a small floor mat. Each group member must hold one corner of the mat. Balance a foam ball in the center of each mat.

Challenge each group to transport their ball through the obstacle course. Kids must hold on to the mat at all times. If a group's ball rolls off the mat, the group should start over. Send kids through the course one group at a time.

Say • Was it hard to carry the ball through the course on the mat? In today's Bible story, four men carried their friend on a mat to see Jesus.

- small floor mats or towels, 1 per group
- foam balls, 1 per group
- masking tape or painter's tape

Tip: When you set up the obstacle course, go through it to ensure kids can complete the course safely.

Transition to large group

Large Group LEADER

Session Title: Four Friends Helped
Bible Passage: Matthew 9:1-8; Mark 2:1-12; Luke 5:17-26
Big Picture Question: How could Jesus forgive people's sins? Jesus was going to take the punishment for sin when He died on the cross.
Key Passage: John 20:30-31
Unit Christ Connection: Jesus' miracles demonstrated His divine authority.

Countdown

• countdown video

Show the countdown video as your kids arrive, and set it to end as large group time begins.

Introduce the session (2 minutes)

• leader attire
• stopwatch

[Large Group Leader enters wearing running shoes. Leader carries a stopwatch around his or her neck and jogs in place for a few seconds.]

Leader • Well, hello! I'm [*your name*], and I was just cooling down from a run. I know, I know. I am trying out *another* sport. But I think I will really like running. The track coach was looking for someone to run in a relay. Three other runners and I take turns running around the track, passing a baton to each other. We all work together as a team. Speaking of teams, today's Bible story is about four friends who worked together. Are you ready for it?

Timeline map (2 minutes)

• Timeline Map

Use the timeline map to point out and review the previous Bible stories: "Jesus Healed an Official's Son," "Jesus Drove Out Evil Spirits," "Jesus Healed Peter's Mother-in-Law," and "Jesus Cleansed a Leper."

Leader • Who can tell me what you remember about these Bible stories? Jesus performed many miracles. *What happened when Jesus performed miracles? Jesus' miracles helped people believe in Him.* Jesus showed He has power over all our enemies when He commanded the evil spirit to go away and it obeyed Him. Last time we learned about Jesus healing a man with a serious skin disease. Our sin is like a disease too. *Who can take away our sin? Jesus can and wants to cleanse us from sin.*

Here is today's Bible story. It's called "Four Friends Helped." Well, that's interesting. Do you think Jesus did a miracle in this story? We'll find out!

Big picture question (1 minute)

Leader • Before we hear the Bible story, let's get ready by looking at this week's big picture question. Here it is: *How could Jesus forgive people's sins?* Interesting. We better listen to the Bible story to figure out what happened. Whose sins did Jesus forgive?

Tell the Bible story (10 minutes)

- "Four Friends Helped" video
- Bibles, 1 per kid
- Bible Story Picture Slide or Poster
- Big Picture Question Slide or Poster

Open your Bible to Matthew 9:1-8; Mark 2:1-12; or Luke 5:17-26. Tell the Bible story in your own words or show the Bible story video "Four Friends Helped."

Leader • Jesus grew up in Nazareth, but when He was an adult, He lived in a city called Capernaum (kuh PUHR nay uhm). One day, when Jesus was home, many people came to hear Him teach. Religious leaders—the Pharisees and other teachers of the law—came. Some of them traveled many miles to hear Jesus. The house was so crowded that no one else could get in.

Then some men came to the house. They carried their friend on a mat because he couldn't walk. They wanted to see Jesus. They hoped Jesus would heal their friend. But the house was too crowded. What did they do? Did they turn around and go home? No! The four friends went up onto the roof, took off the roof above Jesus, and lowered their friend down into the house.

Can you imagine? Jesus was sitting there in front of the crowd and all of a sudden this man came down from the ceiling right in front of Him! Jesus saw that the friends had faith; they trusted that Jesus was telling the truth about who He is and that He could heal their friend.

Then Jesus said something that surprised everyone. He looked at the man on the mat and said, "Young man, your sins are forgiven!" This made the religious leaders upset because they thought Jesus was being disrespectful to God. They knew only God can forgive sins. They didn't realize that Jesus is God's Son.

The Bible says the punishment for sin is death. Everyone who sins deserves to die and spend eternity apart from God, but God sent Jesus to earth to rescue people from sins. Jesus was going to die on the cross to take the punishment for sins. That is why He could forgive people's sins.

How could Jesus forgive people's sins? Jesus was going to take the punishment for sin when He died on the cross. That's our big picture question and answer. Say it with me. *How could Jesus forgive people's sins? Jesus was going to take the punishment for sin when He died on the cross.*

Jesus knew that the religious leaders were upset. So He showed that He has power on earth—not only to forgive sins but to heal a man who couldn't walk. Jesus told the man, "Get up, pick up your mat, and go home." And that is just what the man did.

It was a miracle! The people praised God and said, "We

have never seen anything like this!"

Jesus not only healed the man physically, He forgave the man's sins. Being able to walk would help the man while he was alive on earth, but being forgiven for his sins helped the man eternally. Jesus was going to die to take the punishment for the man's sins, and the man would live with God forever in heaven.

We sin and need forgiveness too. Jesus gives forgiveness and eternal life to those who trust in Him.

The Gospel: God's Plan for Me (optional)

• Bible

Using Scripture and the guide provided, explain to boys and girls how to become a Christian. Tell kids how they can respond, and provide counselors to speak with each kid individually. Guide counselors to use open-ended questions to allow kids to determine the direction of the conversation.

Encourage boys and girls to ask their parents, small group leaders, or other adults any questions they may have about becoming a Christian.

Key passage (5 minutes)

• Key Passage Slide or Poster
• "Written" song

Leader • Jesus' miracles amazed many of the people who witnessed them or heard about them, and many of the people believed in Jesus because of His miracles. That's why the apostle John wrote about Jesus' miracles in the Gospel of John. Can anyone say our key passage, John 20:30-31, from memory?

Invite several volunteers to recite the key passage. Then lead the group to say it together. Ask two or three kids to lead everyone in singing "Written."

• "Unit 26 Session 5" discussion starter video

Discussion starter video (5 minutes)

Leader • The four men who carried their friend to Jesus

had faith. They believed that Jesus could help their friend who could not walk. Helping their friend was probably hard work, but they were determined to get him to Jesus. How willing are you to help someone in need? Let's watch this video.

Show the "Unit 26 Session 5" video.

Leader •What would you do to help the person in need in each of those scenarios?

Invite kids to respond. Encourage them to be willing to help others when they see someone who needs help.

Sing (3 minutes)

• "This is Amazing Grace" song

Leader •Jesus helps us by meeting our greatest need: to be saved from our sins. Let's sing about His amazing grace.

Lead boys and girls to sing "This Is Amazing Grace."

Prayer (2 minutes)

Leader •*How could Jesus forgive people's sins? Jesus was going to take the punishment for sin when He died on the cross.* Great job. Let's pray before you go to small groups.

Lead the kids in prayer. Thank God for sending Jesus to take the punishment for our sins so we can be forgiven. Pray that kids would trust in Jesus for their salvation.

Dismiss to small groups

The Gospel: God's Plan for Me

Ask kids if they have ever heard the word *gospel*. Clarify that the word *gospel* means "good news." It is the message about Christ, the kingdom of God, and salvation. Use the following guide to share the gospel with kids.

God rules. Explain to kids that the Bible tells us God created everything, and He is in charge of everything. Invite a volunteer to read Genesis 1:1 from the Bible. Read Revelation 4:11 or Colossians 1:16-17 aloud and explain what these verses mean.

We sinned. Tell kids that since the time of Adam and Eve, everyone has chosen to disobey God. (Romans 3:23) The Bible calls this sin. Because God is holy, God cannot be around sin. Sin separates us from God and deserves God's punishment of death. (Romans 6:23)

God provided. Choose a child to read John 3:16 aloud. Say that God sent His Son, Jesus, the perfect solution to our sin problem, to rescue us from the punishment we deserve. It's something we, as sinners, could never earn on our own. Jesus alone saves us. Read and explain Ephesians 2:8-9.

Jesus gives. Share with kids that Jesus lived a perfect life, died on the cross for our sins, and rose again. Because Jesus gave up His life for us, we can be welcomed into God's family for eternity. This is the best gift ever! Read Romans 5:8; 2 Corinthians 5:21; or 1 Peter 3:18.

We respond. Tell kids that they can respond to Jesus. Read Romans 10:9-10,13. Review these aspects of our response: Believe in your heart that Jesus alone saves you through what He's already done on the cross. Repent, turning from self and sin to Jesus. Tell God and others that your faith is in Jesus.

Offer to talk with any child who is interested in responding to Jesus.

Small Group LEADER

Session Title: Four Friends Helped
Bible Passage: Matthew 9:1-8; Mark 2:1-12; Luke 5:17-26
Big Picture Question: How could Jesus forgive people's sins? Jesus was going to take the punishment for sin when He died on the cross.
Key Passage: John 20:30-31
Unit Christ Connection: Jesus' miracles demonstrated His divine authority.

Key passage activity (5 minutes)

- Key Passage Poster
- numbered cube

Direct kids to stand in a circle. Display the key passage poster and lead them to read the key passage aloud. Then cover the key passage poster. Invite one kid to toss a numbered cube. Kids should repeat the key passage the number of times indicated on the cube. Encourage them to strive for accuracy, not speed. As time allows, invite another kid to toss the numbered cube and lead kids to continue reciting the passage from memory.

Say • Which of the four Gospels is this passage in? (*John*)
• Which Bible stories are these verses talking about? (*Jesus' miracles*)

Bible story review & Bible skills (10 minutes)

- Bibles, 1 per kid
- Small Group Visual Pack
- paper
- pencils

Review the timeline in the small group visual pack. Challenge kids to name the four books in the Gospels. (*Matthew, Mark, Luke, John*) Retell or review the Bible story in your own words or use the bolded text of the Bible story script.

Invite kids to play a "Sink or Swim" game. Form two teams and instruct each team to stand on opposite sides of the room. Give each team paper and a pencil. Explain that you will ask a review question, and each team should write down an answer. Call for each team to reveal its answer. If a team is incorrect, one of its players must sit. If a team is correct, it may "rescue" a player who is sitting, allowing him to stand again, or it may "sink" a player from the other team, causing him to sit. The team with the most players standing at the end is the winner.

1. In what city did people come to hear Jesus teach? (*Capernaum, Mark 2:1*)

2. How crowded was the house where Jesus preached? (*There was no more room, Mark 2:2*)

3. How many friends carried the man who was paralyzed? (*four friends, Mark 2:3*)

4. Why couldn't the men get to Jesus? (*the crowd was too big; Mark 2:4; Luke 5:19*)

5. How did the men get their friend to Jesus? (*They removed the roof above Jesus and lowered the man down; Mark 2:4; Luke 5:19*)

6. What did Jesus see in the four friends? (*their faith; Matt. 9:2; Mark 2:5; Luke 5:20*)

7. What did the religious leaders accuse Jesus of doing? (*blaspheming, or speaking against God; Matt. 9:3; Mark 2:6-7; Luke 5:21*)

8. What did Jesus tell the paralyzed man to do? (*to get up, pick up his mat, and go home; Matt. 9:6; Mark 2:11; Luke 5:24*)

9. How did the crowd react? (*They were astounded and gave glory to God; Matt. 9:8; Mark 2:12; Luke 5:26*)

10. ***How could Jesus forgive people's sins? Jesus was going to take the punishment for sin when He died on the cross.***

If you choose to review with boys and girls how to become a Christian, explain that kids are welcome to speak with you or another teacher if they have questions.

- **God rules.** God created and is in charge of everything. (Gen. 1:1; Rev. 4:11; Col. 1:16-17)
- **We sinned.** Since Adam and Eve, everyone has chosen to disobey God. (Rom. 3:23; 6:23)
- **God provided.** God sent His Son, Jesus, to rescue us from the punishment we deserve. (John 3:16; Eph. 2:8-9)
- **Jesus gives.** Jesus lived a perfect life, died on the cross for our sins, and rose again so we can be welcomed into God's family. (Rom. 5:8; 2 Cor. 5:21; 1 Pet. 3:18)
- **We respond.** Believe that Jesus alone saves you. Repent. Tell God that your faith is in Jesus. (Rom. 10:9-10,13)

Activity choice (10 minutes)

- rock
- ball of paper
- play dough

Option 1: What's easier?

Set up the following demonstrations. Before each demonstration ask kids to share which task they think is easier to do.

1. **What's easier to move—a rock or a ball of paper?** Position a rock and a ball of paper side-by-side. Choose a volunteer to blow on each object. Which object moves farther?
2. **What's easier to smash—a rock or a ball of play dough?** Give a volunteer a rock and a ball of play dough. Which object is easier to smash?
3. **What's easier to balance—a ball of paper or a ball of play dough?** Choose two volunteers. Challenge one to balance the paper on his finger and the other to balance the play dough.
4. **What's easier to stand on—a rock or a ball of**

paper? Invite a kid to stand on a rock and then a ball of paper. Which object holds up?

Say • Jesus asked the religious leaders, "Which is easier: to say, 'Your sins are forgiven,' or to say, 'Get up and walk'?" How could Jesus prove that the man's sins were forgiven? Jesus proved His power by healing the man who could not walk.

Option 2: I've never seen anything like this!

Form groups of three or four kids. Provide each group with various craft supplies. Invite them to create a new invention. Encourage kids to be creative. Supply scissors, tape, glue, and markers if needed. Give kids several minutes to work. Suggest that kids name their invention, and then invite each group to share. Kids should explain how the invention is used and what it is made of. After a group presents its invention, exclaim, "I've never seen anything like this!"

- scissors
- tape
- glue
- markers
- various supplies: paper towel tubes, aluminum foil, newspaper, drinking straws, sticky notes, paper clips, and so forth

Say • Your inventions are so unique! I've never seen anything like them.

• You know, that's what the people in the crowd said when Jesus forgave the sins of the paralyzed man and then healed him. They said, "We've never seen anything like this!"

• *How could Jesus forgive people's sins? Jesus was going to take the punishment for sin.*

Journal and prayer (5 minutes)

- pencils
- journals
- Bibles
- Journal Page, 1 per kid (enhanced CD)
- "True or False?" activity page, 1 per kid

Say • Write about or draw a picture of a time your friends helped you do something.

Invite kids to share prayer requests. Close the group in prayer, or allow a couple volunteers to close the group in prayer. As time allows, lead kids to complete the activity page "True or False?"

Leader BIBLE STUDY

The Pharisees and scribes were keeping a close eye on Jesus. They watched Him on the Sabbath as He taught in the synagogue. A man there had a paralyzed hand. The religious leaders knew Jesus had power to heal people. They watched to see if He would heal on the Sabbath. According to the law, people should not do work on the Sabbath.

Maybe Jesus had been standing before the crowd when He noticed the religious leaders. He was not only aware of their presence, but He knew their thoughts as well. So Jesus called to the man with the paralyzed hand. "Stand up here," Jesus said. So the man stood, and Jesus addressed the Pharisees and scribes.

"Is it lawful on the Sabbath to do what is good or to do what is evil, to save a life or to kill?" Jesus asked. The religious leaders did not answer. The hardness of their hearts made Jesus sad. They didn't understand God's purpose for the Sabbath. Jesus told the man, "Stretch out your hand." The man's hand was healed. The Pharisees and scribes were angry, and they discussed what they might do to Jesus.

Jesus distinguished Himself as the Lord of the Sabbath. (See Luke 6:5.) That Jesus is Lord means He has control. Jesus has control over everything. But Jesus hadn't come to get rid of the Sabbath; He wanted to remind the people why God gave them the Sabbath. (See Ex. 20:8-11.) God intended for the Sabbath to be a blessing to His people, a day of rest from their hard work. But the Pharisees made the Sabbath all about following the rules, making the Sabbath a burden instead.

The Sabbath is not for our duty but for our delight. Jesus rejected the Pharisees' legalism that made it impossible to do anything on the Sabbath. The Sabbath is a day to focus on Jesus. In Him, we have rest from striving to be good enough. True rest comes when we trust in Jesus' finished work on the cross for our salvation.

Older Kids BIBLE STUDY OVERVIEW

Session Title: Jesus Healed a Man's Hand
Bible Passage: Matthew 12:9-14; Mark 3:1-6; Luke 6:6-11
Big Picture Question: What did Jesus' miracles prove? Jesus' miracles
   proved that He is the Son of God.
Key Passage: John 20:30-31
Unit Christ Connection: Jesus' miracles demonstrated His divine
   authority.

Small Group Opening

Large Group Leader

Small Group Leader

The BIBLE STORY

Jesus Healed a Man's Hand

Matthew 12:9-14; Mark 3:1-6; Luke 6:6-11

On the Sabbath, Jesus went into the synagogue. The Sabbath was a special day—a holy day set apart for God. **God had commanded His people not to do any work on the Sabbath. The Sabbath was a day to rest and worship God.**

Jesus taught the people in the synagogue. One of the men there was unable to move his right hand; it was paralyzed. **Pharisees and teachers of the law were also in the synagogue, and they watched Jesus carefully. They wondered if Jesus was going to heal the man's hand.** These leaders wanted to see what Jesus would do so they could accuse Him of doing something wrong.

"Is it OK to heal people on the Sabbath?" the leaders asked.

Jesus gave the leaders an example. Maybe they could figure out the answer themselves. **Jesus said, "If any of you has a sheep and it falls into a ditch on the Sabbath, wouldn't you grab the sheep and lift it out of the ditch?"** Of course a man wouldn't leave the sheep lying in the ditch; sheep were property, and no man would want to let his sheep get hurt or die.

Then Jesus said, "A man is much more important than a sheep, so it is right to do good on the Sabbath."

Jesus knew that the leaders were hoping to accuse Him of doing the wrong thing, so he **called out to the man with the paralyzed hand. "Stand up here where everyone can see you."**

Then Jesus said to the man, "Stretch out your hand." So the man stretched out his hand. He had not been able to move it before, but now his right hand was just as good as his left.

But instead of being happy for the man or praising God for giving Jesus the power to heal, **the Pharisees and teachers of the law were angry! They left the synagogue and talked among themselves, planning how they might kill Jesus.**

Christ Connection: Jesus showed that God's laws were meant to help people, not to hurt them. Jesus acted in love, even on the Sabbath. The religious leaders planned to kill Jesus. They did not know Jesus was going to die to show God's love to the whole world. God provided forgiveness and salvation through Jesus' death on the cross.

Small Group OPENING

Session Title: Jesus Healed a Man's Hand
Bible Passage: Matthew 12:9-14; Mark 3:1-6; Luke 6:6-11
Big Picture Question: What did Jesus' miracles prove? Jesus' miracles proved that He is the Son of God.
Key Passage: John 20:30-31
Unit Christ Connection: Jesus' miracles demonstrated His divine authority.

Welcome time

Greet each kid as he or she arrives. Use this time to collect the offering, fill out attendance sheets, and help new kids connect to your group.

Choose a few volunteers to share their routines for Sunday afternoons. What do they like to do after they go to church? Adapt your question if kids attend church at a different time during the week.

Activity page (5 minutes)

- "Fill 'er Up!" activity page, 1 per kid
- pencils

Give each kid a "Fill 'er Up!" activity page. Instruct each kid to think about what fills up his or her day. Instruct kids to write their weekly schedules on the agenda page. They should include before- and after-school activities, chores, and other scheduled events.

When kids finish, guide them to look over their weekly schedules. Choose two or three volunteers to share their schedules with the group.

Say • Who thinks they have the busiest schedule? What day of the week is busiest for you? Which day is least busy? Do you wish your schedule was less busy?
Invite kids to share their answers.

Session starter (10 minutes)

Option 1: Non-dominate challenge

Challenge each kid to complete each of the following tasks with his or her non-dominate hand. (Kids who are right-handed should use their left hands, and vice versa.)

1. Write your name on a piece of paper.
2. Draw a circle around your name.
3. Erase the last letter of your name.
4. Underline the first letter of your name.
5. Draw your favorite animal on the back of the paper.

As time allows, continue giving tasks for kids to complete.

Say • Was it a challenge to use your non-dominate hand? Today we are going to hear a Bible story about a man who could not use one of his hands.

Option 2: Rules that help

Allow kids to work together as one large group or form a few small groups. Give each group a piece of paper and a marker. Instruct each group to come up with a list of five rules that they think are most important for a classroom.

After several minutes, call on each group to share its list.

Say • How did you decide which rules are most important? Are the rules you wrote down helpful to everyone? Are there ever times it is OK to not follow these rules? Do you think having rules is a good idea?

• God gave His people rules in the Bible about how to live. Do you know any of the Ten Commandments? God gave His people laws to help them. Today we are going to hear a Bible story about a lesson Jesus taught to some men who had strong opinions about always following the rules.

Transition to large group

• paper
• pencils

• large pieces of paper
• markers

Large Group LEADER

Session Title: Jesus Healed a Man's Hand
Bible Passage: Matthew 12:9-14; Mark 3:1-6; Luke 6:6-11
Big Picture Question: What did Jesus' miracles prove? Jesus' miracles proved that He is the Son of God.
Key Passage: John 20:30-31
Unit Christ Connection: Jesus' miracles demonstrated His divine authority.

Countdown

• countdown video

Show the countdown video as your kids arrive, and set it to end as large group time begins.

Introduce the session (2 minutes)

• leader attire
• beach towel

[Large Group Leader enters wearing swim goggles and carrying a beach towel.]

Leader • Hi, everyone! You're back! I was just getting ready to go to the pool later. I am thinking about trying out for the swim team. I've tried a lot of different sports over the past few weeks, and I'm positive swimming is for me. Have you ever noticed how many rules are at a swimming pool? The lifeguards are always telling me, "No running!" or "No diving!"

Hey, that reminds me of today's Bible story. It's about Jesus and a lesson He taught some men who had the wrong idea about God's laws. Let's get started.

Timeline map (2 minutes)

• Timeline Map

Use the timeline map to point out and review the previous Bible stories: "Jesus Healed an Official's Son," "Jesus Drove Out Evil Spirits," "Jesus Healed Peter's Mother-in-Law," "Jesus Cleansed a Leper," and "Four Friends Helped."

Leader • We have covered a lot of Bible stories these last few weeks! All of these stories are about miraculous things Jesus did—healing a boy from miles away, commanding an evil spirit to go away, healing a woman with a fever, healing a man with a skin disease, and healing a man who could not walk. Today's Bible story is called "Jesus Healed a Man's Hand." That sounds like another miracle!

Big picture question (1 minute)

Leader • I need you to listen very carefully to the Bible story so you can help me answer our big picture question. This week, our big picture question is, ***What did Jesus' miracles prove?***

Tell the Bible story (10 minutes)

- "Jesus Healed a Man's Hand" video
- Bibles, 1 per kid
- Bible Story Picture Slide or Poster
- Big Picture Question Slide or Poster

Open your Bible to Matthew 12:9-14; Mark 3:1-6; or Luke 6:6-11. Tell the Bible story in your own words or show the Bible story video "Jesus Healed a Man's Hand."

Leader • Jesus went to the synagogue on the Sabbath. Can anyone tell me what was special about the Sabbath? (*The Sabbath was a holy day set apart for God. God had commanded His people not to do any work on the Sabbath. It was a day to rest and worship God.*)

One of the men in the synagogue could not move his hand; it was paralyzed. People knew that Jesus had the power to heal; they had seen Him do it or had heard stories about the miraculous things He had done. So the religious leaders in the synagogue watched Jesus. They wanted to see if Jesus would heal the man's hand—not because they cared about the man and wanted him to be healed but because they wanted to accuse Jesus of doing something wrong.

Was it wrong for Jesus to heal on the Sabbath? That's what the religious leaders asked Jesus. They said, "Is it OK to heal people on the Sabbath?"

Jesus could have just told them the answer, but He wanted to teach them a lesson. So Jesus asked them a question to see if they could figure out what was the right thing to do. Jesus asked the leaders, "If you had a sheep and the sheep fell into a ditch on the Sabbath, would you lift it out of the ditch?"

Of course! No one would just leave his sheep in a ditch to get hurt or even die. So Jesus told them that people are more important than sheep. He said that it is right to do good on the Sabbath.

Jesus told the man with the paralyzed hand to stand up. Then He said, "Stretch out your hand." The man stretched out his hand! He was healed! A miracle! *What did Jesus' miracles prove? Jesus' miracles proved that He is the Son of God.* That's our big picture question and answer. Let's say it together. *What did Jesus' miracles prove? Jesus' miracles proved that He is the Son of God.*

The religious leaders were not happy about Jesus' miracle. They did not praise God for the wonderful thing Jesus had done. Instead, they left angry, and they made a plan about how they might kill Jesus.

Did you know that even though the religious leaders made a plan to kill Jesus, God's plan all along was for Jesus to die? God sent Jesus into the world to rescue people from sin. Jesus died on the cross to take the punishment for sin, and then He rose from the dead. When we trust in Jesus, God forgives us for our sin and we will live with Him forever in heaven.

The Gospel: God's Plan for Me (optional)

Using Scripture and the guide provided, explain to boys and girls how to become a Christian. Tell kids how they can respond, and provide counselors to speak with each kid individually. Encourage boys and girls to ask their parents, small group leaders, or other adults any questions they may have about becoming a Christian.

Key passage (5 minutes)

- Key Passage Slide or Poster
- "Written" song

Leader •This is the last week we will be studying our key passage, John 20:30-31. Does everyone have it memorized? If not, keeping working on it. If so, great job! I know you have all been working very hard.

Lead boys and girls to recite the key passage from memory. Then call on volunteers to answer the following questions:

1. Who wrote this passage? (*the apostle John*)
2. What does the key passage explain? (*why the stories of Jesus' miracles are written in the Gospel of John*)
3. **What did Jesus' miracles prove? Jesus' miracles proved that He is the Son of God.**

Leader •The stories of Jesus' miracles are written in the Bible so that we will read them and believe that Jesus is the Messiah, the Son of God. Do you believe that?

Sing "Written."

Discussion starter video (5 minutes)

- "Unit 26 Session 6" discussion starter video

Leader •The religious leaders in today's Bible story had some strong opinions about what people should and should not do on the Sabbath. Remember, the Sabbath is a special day—a holy day set apart for God. God had commanded His people not to do any work on the Sabbath. The Sabbath is a day to rest and worship God.

Were the religious leaders right? Watch this.

Show the "Unit 26 Session 6" video.

Leader •Are these things allowed on the Sabbath? Is it OK to cook food or give your dog a bath or talk on the phone on the Sabbath?

Jesus showed that God's laws were meant to help people, not to hurt them. He acted in love by doing a miracle and healing the man's hand on the Sabbath. *What did Jesus' miracles prove? Jesus' miracles proved that He is the Son of God.*

Sing (3 minutes)

• "This Is Amazing Grace" song

Leader •When God gave His people the laws like the Ten Commandments, they showed how God wants people to live holy lives. People tried hard to obey God's laws, but everyone disobeyed Him. That's called sin.

God's law about the Sabbath is not to keep us from doing anything on the Sabbath like the religious leaders thought. God gives us the Sabbath to help us. He wants us to rest and think about Jesus. On the Sabbath, we can remember that we don't have to be perfect. Jesus lived a perfect life for us and died on the cross for our sins. He rose from the dead, and we can trust in Him for our salvation. Let's sing.

Lead boys and girls to sing "This Is Amazing Grace."

Prayer (2 minutes)

Leader •Let's pray before you go to your small groups. Lead the kids in prayer. Pray that kids will rest in Jesus' finished work on the cross instead of striving to be good enough. Thank Jesus for rescuing us from our sins.

Dismiss to small groups

The Gospel: God's Plan for Me

Ask kids if they have ever heard the word *gospel*. Clarify that the word *gospel* means "good news." It is the message about Christ, the kingdom of God, and salvation. Use the following guide to share the gospel with kids.

God rules. Explain to kids that the Bible tells us God created everything, and He is in charge of everything. Invite a volunteer to read Genesis 1:1 from the Bible. Read Revelation 4:11 or Colossians 1:16-17 aloud and explain what these verses mean.

We sinned. Tell kids that since the time of Adam and Eve, everyone has chosen to disobey God. (Romans 3:23) The Bible calls this sin. Because God is holy, God cannot be around sin. Sin separates us from God and deserves God's punishment of death. (Romans 6:23)

God provided. Choose a child to read John 3:16 aloud. Say that God sent His Son, Jesus, the perfect solution to our sin problem, to rescue us from the punishment we deserve. It's something we, as sinners, could never earn on our own. Jesus alone saves us. Read and explain Ephesians 2:8-9.

Jesus gives. Share with kids that Jesus lived a perfect life, died on the cross for our sins, and rose again. Because Jesus gave up His life for us, we can be welcomed into God's family for eternity. This is the best gift ever! Read Romans 5:8; 2 Corinthians 5:21; or 1 Peter 3:18.

We respond. Tell kids that they can respond to Jesus. Read Romans 10:9-10,13. Review these aspects of our response: Believe in your heart that Jesus alone saves you through what He's already done on the cross. Repent, turning from self and sin to Jesus. Tell God and others that your faith is in Jesus.

Offer to talk with any child who is interested in responding to Jesus.

Small Group LEADER

Session Title: Jesus Healed a Man's Hand
Bible Passage: Matthew 12:9-14; Mark 3:1-6; Luke 6:6-11
Big Picture Question: What did Jesus' miracles prove? Jesus' miracles proved that He is the Son of God.
Key Passage: John 20:30-31
Unit Christ Connection: Jesus' miracles demonstrated His divine authority.

Key passage activity (5 minutes)

- Key Passage Poster

Direct kids to stand in a circle. Lead them to say the key passage together one time. Then choose one player to begin. The first player will say as many or as few words of the key passage as he wants. When he pauses, the player to his right picks up where he left off. The second player says one or more words. When she pauses, the third player begins.

Continue around the circle. If a player does not know the next word, he should sit down. Play continues until kids have recited the entire verse. Then invite any sitting players to stand and play again.

Say • Great job! You have done so well memorizing the key passage. John 20:30-31 is a reminder of why these stories about Jesus' miracles are in the Bible. Jesus performed many more miraculous signs than the ones we read about in the Bible, but these are written so that we may believe that Jesus is the Messiah, the Son of God.

- Bibles, 1 per kid
- Small Group Visual Pack
- "Review Hands" (enhanced CD)
- colored paper
- yarn or string
- scissors
- tape

Bible story review & Bible skills (10 minutes)

Before class, print a set of "Review Hands" onto colored paper and cut them out. If your group is large, prepare more than one set and let kids play in small groups.

Review the timeline in the small group visual pack. Retell or review the Bible story in your own words or use the bolded text of the Bible story script.

Form groups of three to five kids. For each group, mix up a set of review hands and tape the hands on the floor in one area of the room. Provide the group with scissors, tape, and yarn or string. Challenge kids in each group to work together to connect each left-hand question with the correct right-hand answer. When kids finish, review the questions and answers together.

1. What was wrong with the man at the synagogue? (*His right hand was paralyzed; Matt. 12:10; Mark 3:3; Luke 6:6*)

2. Who watched Jesus to see if He did something wrong? (*The Pharisees and scribes, or teachers of the law; Luke 6:7*)

3. What did Jesus tell the man to do? (*to stretch out his hand; Matt. 12:13; Mark 3:5; Luke 6:10*)

4. How did the Pharisees and teachers of the law react to Jesus' miracle? (*They were angry and planned to kill Jesus; Matt. 12:14; Mark 3:6; Luke 6:11*)

5. **What did Jesus' miracles prove? Jesus' miracles proved that He is the Son of God.**

If you choose to review with boys and girls how to become a Christian, explain that kids are welcome to speak with you or another teacher if they have questions.

- **God rules.** God created and is in charge of everything. (Gen. 1:1; Rev. 4:11; Col. 1:16-17)
- **We sinned.** Since Adam and Eve, everyone has chosen to disobey God. (Rom. 3:23; 6:23)
- **God provided.** God sent His Son, Jesus, to rescue us from the punishment we deserve. (John 3:16; Eph. 2:8-9)
- **Jesus gives.** Jesus lived a perfect life, died on the

cross for our sins, and rose again so we can be welcomed into God's family. (Rom. 5:8; 2 Cor. 5:21; 1 Pet. 3:18)

- **We respond.** Believe that Jesus alone saves you. Repent. Tell God that your faith is in Jesus. (Rom. 10:9-10,13)

Activity choice (10 minutes)

- cotton balls
- plastic cups

Option 1: Gather the herd

Form two teams. Instruct each team to stand in a circle. Choose one player on each team to stand in the middle of the circle. Give the player in the middle a plastic cup to hold over her head. Give each of the other players a handful of cotton balls. Guide the players to stand so that they are about six feet from the player in the center. Explain that the cotton balls represent sheep. Any "sheep" not in the cup ("pen") is "in the ditch." Players should try to get all of the sheep out of the ditch and into the pen.

When you say go, players should try tossing their cotton balls into the plastic cup on the middle player's head. Players may take turns or they may toss all their cotton balls at the same time. Players may pick up cotton balls that did not land in the cup and try again.

After a couple minutes, call for kids to stop. Count the cotton balls in each cup to see which team gathered the most. If time allows, choose new players to stand in the middle and play again.

Say • Jesus asked the religious leaders about sheep in order to teach them a lesson about doing good on the Sabbath. The religious leaders thought it was OK to pull a sheep out of a ditch on the Sabbath. People are more valuable than sheep! Jesus wanted the religious leaders to know that God made the law about the

Sabbath to help people, not to hurt them. Jesus said it is right to do good on the Sabbath.

Option 2: Handprint prayer cards

- construction paper
- scissors
- markers
- hole punch
- binder rings

Invite kids to make handprint prayer cards. Give each kid a few sheets of construction paper. Guide kids to trace their hands on the construction paper and cut out the hand shapes. Encourage each kid to cut out four or five shapes. Punch a hole in the bottom of each shape and use a binder ring to connect the hands.

Instruct kids to write on each of their handprints the name of a friend or family member they can pray for. Encourage them to include people who might be sick or lonely or who do not know Jesus as Lord and Savior.

Say • Each week on your way to or from church, read through your prayer cards and pray for the people whose names you wrote on the hands.

• Remember that it is right to do good on the Sabbath. God gives us the Sabbath as a day to rest and think about Jesus. Jesus lived a perfect life and died on the cross for our sins. We can trust in Him for salvation.

Journal and prayer (5 minutes)

- pencils
- journals
- Bibles
- Journal Page, 1 per kid (enhanced CD)
- "Gospel Game Plan" activity page, 1 per kid

Lead kids to respond in their journals to the following question: "What was wrong with the way the religious leaders thought about the Sabbath?"

Say • *What did Jesus' miracles prove? Jesus' miracles proved that He is the Son of God.*

Invite kids to share prayer requests. Close the group in prayer, or allow a couple volunteers to close the group in prayer. As time allows, lead kids to complete the activity page "Gospel Game Plan."

Unit 27: JESUS PREACHED

Big Picture Questions

Session 1:
What did Jesus teach in His Sermon on the Mount? Jesus taught how believers should live.

Session 2:
How do people respond to the gospel? Some people believe the gospel and others reject the gospel.

Session 3:
What does it mean to be lost? Being lost means not knowing Jesus as Lord and Savior.

Unit 27: JESUS PREACHED

Unit Description: Jesus preached to many people so they could learn about God. Jesus taught how believers should live, and He told parables about the kingdom of God. He showed that God wants His people to be saved from sin.

Unit Key Passage:
Matthew 6:33

Unit Christ Connection:
Jesus taught people that the kingdom of God had come and that salvation is available to all.

Session 1:
The Sermon on the Mount
Matthew 5–7

Session 2:
Parable of the Sower
Matthew 13:1-23; Mark 4:1-20; Luke 8:4-15

Session 3:
Three Parables
Luke 15

Leader BIBLE STUDY

During His time on earth, Jesus spent time preaching about God's kingdom. One of Jesus' most well-known sermons is the Sermon on the Mount. On that day, crowds of people had come to hear Jesus. Jesus went up on a mountain in Galilee, and He sat down and began to teach.

Jesus' Sermon on the Mount is recorded across three chapters in the Gospel of Matthew. In Matthew 5–7, Jesus taught how believers should live. While Matthew 5:1-2 specifies that Jesus taught His disciples, Matthew 7:28 reveals that the crowds listened to His sermon as well.

First, Jesus began with the Beatitudes. The Beatitudes describe God's great blessings for believers. God's kingdom belongs to the spiritually needy, God will comfort those who are sad, and God will give mercy to those who show mercy to others. Jesus gives believers reason to be glad when life on earth is hard because great rewards await in heaven.

Jesus also taught how believers should live in a world that does not honor Him. Jesus called believers "the salt of the earth" and "the light of the world" (Matt. 5:13-14). He said the good works of His followers should cause others to give glory to God.

Jesus taught about a righteousness that comes from the inside. God's people had the law of Moses, but some of them—the Pharisees, in particular—were concerned mostly with the appearance of being righteous. They tried hard to look righteous on the outside, but it was all an act. Jesus warned against hypocrites, people who pretend to be something they're not. When a person knows and loves Jesus, he or she has a changed heart that wants to honor Jesus.

As you teach kids Jesus' Sermon on the Mount, emphasize that this moral teaching was not a list of requirements for being accepted by God. Rather, Jesus described what a person's life looks like when he or she follows Jesus and lives to honor Him. God's standards remind us that we rely on His grace through the gift of salvation in His Son.

Older Kids BIBLE STUDY OVERVIEW

Session Title: The Sermon on the Mount
Bible Passage: Matthew 5–7
Big Picture Question: What did Jesus teach in His Sermon on the Mount? Jesus taught how believers should live.
Key Passage: Matthew 6:33
Unit Christ Connection: Jesus taught people that the kingdom of God had come and that salvation is available to all.

Small Group Opening

Large Group Leader

Small Group Leader

The BIBLE STORY

The Sermon on the Mount
Matthew 5–7

Great crowds followed Jesus wherever He went. The people were curious about Jesus, and they wanted to hear Him teach. **One day, Jesus went up on a mountain. He sat down and began to teach His disciples about the kingdom of God.** Jesus taught the people how to live, how to treat each other, and how to love God.

First, Jesus taught about the blessings of believing in Him. He said:
"The poor in spirit are blessed, for the kingdom of heaven is theirs.
Those who mourn are blessed, for they will be comforted.
The gentle are blessed, for they will inherit the earth.
Those who hunger and thirst for righteousness are blessed, for they will be filled.
The merciful are blessed, for they will be shown mercy.
The pure in heart are blessed, for they will see God.
The peacemakers are blessed, for they will be called sons of God.
Those who are persecuted for righteousness are blessed, for the kingdom of heaven is theirs."

Then Jesus taught how believers should live. Jesus said that believers are the light of the world. **"Let your light shine before others so that they may see the good things you do and choose to praise God."**

Jesus said that He came not to do away with the law, but to obey it. To enter heaven, a person can't just look righteous on the outside—like the scribes and the Pharisees. A person must be righteous on the inside too.

Jesus taught the people how to follow Him. He taught them how they should live.

"Love your enemies, and pray for them," Jesus said.

"Whenever you give to the poor, give in secret. And when you pray, don't pray just so that people will hear you." **Jesus also taught the people how to pray.**

Jesus taught people about forgiveness. "Forgive others," He said. "If

you forgive those who sin against you, God will forgive you as well. But if you don't forgive them, God will not forgive you."

Jesus said, "Don't collect treasures on earth, which can be destroyed or stolen. Collect treasures in heaven instead. For where your treasure is, that's where your heart will be also."

Jesus also taught that God provides for His people. "Don't worry about your life or what you will eat or drink or wear. Look at the birds: They don't plant or gather food into barns, yet God feeds them. Aren't you worth more than birds? Seek the kingdom of God and His righteousness first, and all these things that you need will be given to you."

Jesus taught the people many things. When He finished teaching, the crowds were amazed because He taught them like one who had authority, and not like their scribes.

Christ Connection: The scribes and Pharisees looked righteous on the outside, but Jesus taught His disciples about a righteousness that comes from the inside. People who know and love Jesus have changed hearts that want to honor Jesus.

Small Group OPENING

Session Title: The Sermon on the Mount
Bible Passage: Matthew 5–7
Big Picture Question: What did Jesus teach in His Sermon on the Mount? Jesus taught how believers should live.
Key Passage: Matthew 6:33
Unit Christ Connection: Jesus taught people that the kingdom of God had come and that salvation is available to all.

Welcome time

Greet each kid as he or she arrives. Use this time to collect the offering, fill out attendance sheets, and help new kids connect to your group.

Guide kids to discuss what they do when they encounter someone who is mean. How do they react? Lead kids to think about how God wants them to react to someone who is mean.

Activity page (5 minutes)

• "Words on the Mount" activity page, 1 per kid
• pencils

Invite kids to work individually or in pairs to complete the activity page "Words on the Mount." The word search contains 14 words from today's Bible story.

Say • Can anyone guess what today's Bible story is about? Who do you think was teaching? Where was He teaching? We'll find out soon if you're correct!

Session starter (10 minutes)

Option 1: Part of the crowd

Instruct kids to mingle as one big crowd. Call out one of the following commands to form kids into groups. Any kid left out of a group should sit down. Direct kids to continue mingling between commands. After a few rounds, invite the kids who are sitting to join back in the game.

1. Form groups of two.
2. Find two other kids with the same eye color as you.
3. Find one other kid who is the same age as you.
4. Find one other kid who has the same pet as you.

Continue play as time allows. You may supply your own commands relating to kids' characteristics or experiences.

Say • In today's Bible story, Jesus sat on a mountain to teach. A crowd of all sorts of people came to listen to what Jesus had to say.

Option 2: Not what it seems

• 3 various product boxes
• 3 various objects: small foam ball, stapler, plastic cup, or so forth

Before small group, place three various objects in separate product boxes. For example, put a stapler in a box for a toaster, a small foam ball in a box for blocks, and a plastic cup in a box for a hair dryer.

Display the boxes where kids can see them. Call on kids to guess what is inside each box. After several guesses, choose a volunteer to open each box and reveal the object inside. Did any of the kids guess correctly?

Say • From the outside, it looked like certain things were in these boxes, but when you opened them, you saw that other things were inside. That's what the religious leaders were like. They looked good by what they did on the outside, but Jesus knew their hearts were not right on the inside.

• In today's Bible story, Jesus taught how believers should live. Jesus' teaching surprised the religious leaders because they thought they could be good enough to enter God's kingdom.

Transition to large group

Large Group LEADER

Session Title: The Sermon on the Mount
Bible Passage: Matthew 5–7
Big Picture Question: What did Jesus teach in His Sermon on the Mount? Jesus taught how believers should live.
Key Passage: Matthew 6:33
Unit Christ Connection: Jesus taught people that the kingdom of God had come and that salvation is available to all.

• room decorations

Tip: Select decorations that fit your ministry and budget.

Suggested Theme Decorating Ideas: Decorate a focal wall to look like a dock or a boathouse. Hang blue paper near the floor to look like a lake. Cut tree and bush shapes from green paper and attach to the wall. Position props along the wall such as boat oars, fishing nets, fishing poles, life jackets, a tackle box, and so forth.

Countdown

• countdown video

Show the countdown video as your kids arrive, and set it to end as large group time begins.

Introduce the session (2 minutes)

• life jacket
• boat oar
• Bible

[Large Group Leader enters wearing a life jacket. Leader carries a boat oar and a Bible.]

Leader • Hello, everyone! I'm [*your name*]. I'm glad to see you today. You're just in time to join me for my daily Bible study. See, I've been working at this boathouse for a couple years and every day I get some time to myself. I like to take a little boat out on the lake and read my Bible. I love the Bible! It tells us all about God's plan to rescue people from sin. Today I'm starting to read about some of Jesus' sermons. Will you join me?

Timeline map (2 minutes)

• Timeline Map

Point out today's Bible story, "The Sermon on the Mount," on the timeline map.

Leader • This timeline map helps me keep track of what I've learned about so far and what I'll learn about next. You can see that we are right here. The next few weeks, we will learn about some times that Jesus preached. Today's Bible story is called "The Sermon on the Mount." You might already know that *mount* is just another word for "mountain." So Jesus gave a sermon on a mountain. Cool! I love mountains.

Big picture question (1 minute)

Leader • Now, I wonder what Jesus taught on the mountain. Actually, that's our big picture question today. *What did Jesus teach in His Sermon on the Mount?* Listen carefully to the Bible story to see if you can figure out the answer.

Tell the Bible story (10 minutes)

• "The Sermon on the Mount" video
• Bibles, 1 per kid
• Bible Story Picture Slide or Poster
• Big Picture Question Slide or Poster

Tip: A Bible story script is provided at the beginning of every session. Use it to guide you as you prepare to teach the Bible story in your own words. For a shorter version of the Bible story, read only the bold text.

Open your Bible to Matthew 5–7 and tell the Bible story in your own words, or show the Bible story video "The Sermon on the Mount."

Leader • Crowds of people followed Jesus around. The people wanted to hear Him teach about God's kingdom. One of the times Jesus taught, He sat down on a mountain. This teaching is called the Sermon on the Mount. Jesus' Sermon on the Mount is three chapters long—Matthew 5, 6, and 7 in the Bible.

The first thing Jesus taught in His sermon was that people who believe in Him are blessed. The things Jesus said were unusual. He said that people who are poor in spirit are blessed because the kingdom of heaven is theirs.

That means that people who know they need God are blessed. Some people might think that people who are independent—who don't need anyone but themselves—are blessed. But Jesus said that the opposite is true.

Jesus taught how people who believe in Him should live. He said believers are like a light in a dark world. Believers should do good things so that others will see them and praise God. He said that believers should love their enemies and pray for them.

Jesus also said something that surprised the religious leaders. Jesus said that to enter God's kingdom, a person has to be more righteous than the religious leaders! The religious leaders thought they were very good. They tried hard to obey God's laws. But Jesus knew that even though they did good things on the outside, their hearts were not right on the inside. No one's heart is right on the inside. We do not love God like we should. The good news is that Jesus is perfectly righteous. He obeyed God completely and never sinned. Because Jesus died on the cross to take the punishment we deserve for our sin, we can trust in Him and God gives us His righteousness. God changes our hearts so we know and honor Jesus.

Jesus also told the people not to worry. He said that God takes care of the birds and the flowers, and people are worth much more than animals and plants. God will take care of people too.

Jesus taught many things in His Sermon on the Mount. When He was done teaching, the people were amazed. So, *What did Jesus teach in His Sermon on the Mount? Jesus taught how believers should live.* That's our big picture question and answer. Say it with me. *What did Jesus teach in His Sermon on the Mount? Jesus taught how believers should live.*

The Gospel: God's Plan for Me (optional)

Bible

Using Scripture and the guide provided, explain to boys and girls how to become a Christian. Tell kids how they can respond, and provide counselors to speak with each kid individually. Guide counselors to use open-ended questions to allow kids to determine the direction of the conversation.

Encourage boys and girls to ask their parents, small group leaders, or other adults any questions they may have about becoming a Christian.

Key passage (5 minutes)

• Key Passage Slide or Poster
• "Seek Ye First" song

Show the key passage poster and lead kids to read the key passage loud together.

Leader • Have you ever heard this verse before? Jesus said these words in His Sermon on the Mount. Jesus was saying that we should care most about God's kingdom and doing what God wants us to do—knowing and loving Jesus, obeying God, and telling others about Him. God will take care of us and give us everything we need.

Let's work on memorizing our key passage with a song. Lead kids to sing "Seek Ye First" song.

Discussion starter video (5 minutes)

• "Unit 27 Session 1" discussion starter video

Leader • Do you ever have trouble making the right decision? How do you know what is the right thing to do? Think about these scenarios. What would you do? Show the "Unit 27 Session 1" video.

Leader • *What did Jesus teach in His Sermon on the Mount? Jesus taught how believers should live.* The things Jesus taught about how believers should live might not make any sense to people who don't know and love Jesus. Think about the things Jesus taught. Lead kids to consider Jesus' commands such as loving your enemies, forgiving others, and not storing up treasures on earth. Prompt a discussion about why believers can love their enemies, forgive others, or trust God for their needs.

Explain that we were enemies of God, but God loved us and sent Jesus to die for our sins. We can forgive others because Jesus forgave us. We don't have to cling to things like money and possessions on earth because we know that believers have a reward in heaven.

Sing (3 minutes)

• "We Are" song

Leader • Jesus said in His Sermon on the Mount that believers are the light of the world. Think about a light shining in a dark place. That's what we can be like when we tell others the truth about Jesus. Jesus came into the world to save people from their sin. Those who trust in Him will live with God forever in heaven. That's what our theme song is about. Will you sing it with me?
Lead boys and girls to sing "We Are."

Prayer (2 minutes)

Leader • Before you go to your small groups, let's pray.

Father God, thank You for sending Jesus into the world to rescue people from sin. Thank You for His teachings so we know how to live. Lord, we confess that like the religious leaders we may do good things but our hearts are not always right. Please change our hearts so we will want to honor You in all we do. We love You. Amen.

Dismiss to small groups

The Gospel: God's Plan for Me

Ask kids if they have ever heard the word *gospel*. Clarify that the word *gospel* means "good news." It is the message about Christ, the kingdom of God, and salvation. Use the following guide to share the gospel with kids.

God rules. Explain to kids that the Bible tells us God created everything, and He is in charge of everything. Invite a volunteer to read Genesis 1:1 from the Bible. Read Revelation 4:11 or Colossians 1:16-17 aloud and explain what these verses mean.

We sinned. Tell kids that since the time of Adam and Eve, everyone has chosen to disobey God. (Romans 3:23) The Bible calls this sin. Because God is holy, God cannot be around sin. Sin separates us from God and deserves God's punishment of death. (Romans 6:23)

God provided. Choose a child to read John 3:16 aloud. Say that God sent His Son, Jesus, the perfect solution to our sin problem, to rescue us from the punishment we deserve. It's something we, as sinners, could never earn on our own. Jesus alone saves us. Read and explain Ephesians 2:8-9.

Jesus gives. Share with kids that Jesus lived a perfect life, died on the cross for our sins, and rose again. Because Jesus gave up His life for us, we can be welcomed into God's family for eternity. This is the best gift ever! Read Romans 5:8; 2 Corinthians 5:21; or 1 Peter 3:18.

We respond. Tell kids that they can respond to Jesus. Read Romans 10:9-10,13. Review these aspects of our response: Believe in your heart that Jesus alone saves you through what He's already done on the cross. Repent, turning from self and sin to Jesus. Tell God and others that your faith is in Jesus.

Offer to talk with any child who is interested in responding to Jesus.

Small Group LEADER

Session Title: The Sermon on the Mount
Bible Passage: Matthew 5–7
Big Picture Question: What did Jesus teach in His Sermon on the Mount? Jesus taught how believers should live.
Key Passage: Matthew 6:33
Unit Christ Connection: Jesus taught people that the kingdom of God had come and that salvation is available to all.

Key passage activity (5 minutes)

• Key Passage Poster

Display the key passage poster and lead kids to read the key passage together a few times. Then conceal the poster. Read one or two words and then pause for kids to supply the next word. Then continue, pausing occasionally until you have read the entire passage.

Say • Great job. You will have this key passage memorized in no time.

• Remember that Jesus said these words in His Sermon on the Mount. *What did Jesus teach in His Sermon on the Mount? Jesus taught how believers should live.*

Bible story review & Bible skills (10 minutes)

• Bibles, 1 per kid
• Small Group Visual Pack
• index cards
• marker
• tape
• clean flyswatters, 2

Review the timeline in the small group visual pack. Guide kids to find Matthew 5 in their Bibles. Ask them which division of the Bible the Book of Matthew is in. (*Gospels*) Retell or review the Bible story in your own words or use the bolded text of the Bible story script.

Before class, write the following answers on separate index cards. Mix them up and tape them to a wall. Invite two volunteers to play a review game. Give each volunteer a clean flyswatter. Read a review question and challenge each volunteer to swat the correct answer card. For each question, invite two new volunteers to play.

1. ***What did Jesus teach in His Sermon on the Mount? Jesus taught how believers should live.***

2. Where did Jesus teach His sermon? (*on the mountain, Matt. 5:1*)

3. Who did Jesus say is the light of the world? (*believers, Matt. 5:14*)

4. How did Jesus say believers should treat their enemies? (*love them and pray for them, Matt. 5:44*)

5. Who did Jesus say will forgive you if you forgive others? (*God, Matt. 6:14*)

6. Where did Jesus say people should collect treasures? (*in heaven, Matt. 6:20*)

7. Who provides everything we need? (*God; Matt. 6:30,33*)

8. Why were the crowds amazed at Jesus' teaching? (*Jesus taught like one who had authority, Matt. 7:28-29*)

If you choose to review with boys and girls how to become a Christian, explain that kids are welcome to speak with you or another teacher if they have questions.

- **God rules.** God created and is in charge of everything. (Gen. 1:1; Rev. 4:11; Col. 1:16-17)
- **We sinned.** Since Adam and Eve, everyone has chosen to disobey God. (Rom. 3:23; 6:23)
- **God provided.** God sent His Son, Jesus, to rescue us from the punishment we deserve. (John 3:16; Eph. 2:8-9)
- **Jesus gives.** Jesus lived a perfect life, died on the cross for our sins, and rose again so we can be welcomed into God's family. (Rom. 5:8; 2 Cor. 5:21; 1 Pet. 3:18)

• **We respond.** Believe that Jesus alone saves you. Repent. Tell God that your faith is in Jesus. (Rom. 10:9-10,13)

Activity choice (10 minutes)

Option 1: Up, down, stop, go

Direct kids to stand around the room. Make sure each kid has ample space to move in place. Invite kids to play an opposites game. Explain that you will give a command: *up*, *down*, *stop*, or *go*. For each command, kids must do the opposite. If you say "up," kids should kneel down. If you say "down," kids should raise their hands above their heads. If you say "stop," kids should run in place. If you say "go," kids should stand still.

Play a practice round for kids to try out the commands. If a kid does not do the opposite of the command you give, he should sit down. Play until only a few players remain. Then invite everyone to join in for another round. You may choose to invite a volunteer to give the commands, or you may challenge kids by giving the commands more quickly.

Say • Some of the things Jesus taught in His Sermon on the Mount are the opposite of what we usually want to do. Jesus did not say to hate your enemies; He said to love them. Jesus did not say to hold a grudge against people who wrong you; He said to forgive them. Jesus did not say to fill your bank account with money; He said not to collect treasures on earth.

• Jesus taught how believers should live. Believers should live differently than those who do not know and love Jesus.

• black, red, and pink construction paper
• scissors
• glue sticks
• markers

Option 2: Changed heart mosaics

Cut several heart shapes from black construction paper.

Give each kid one or more heart shapes. Supply red and pink construction paper.

Instruct kids to tear the red and pink paper into small pieces. Demonstrate how to glue the pieces over the heart shape to make a mosaic. Encourage kids to use the red and pink pieces to completely cover their heart shapes.

Say • Jesus taught how believers should live. He said that the way the Pharisees and religious leaders lived wasn't good enough to enter God's kingdom. They did good things on the outside, but their hearts were not right on the inside.

• We aren't good enough to enter God's kingdom either because we sin. But Jesus came to save us from sin. When we trust in Him, He takes away our sin and gives us His righteousness. He changes our hearts so that we will want to honor Him in all that we do.

Allow the heart shapes to dry and then direct kids to write *Matthew 6:33* on them. Suggest kids keep the hearts in their Bibles as a reminder that people who know and love Jesus have changed hearts.

Journal and prayer (5 minutes)

- pencils
- journals
- Bibles
- Journal Page, 1 per kid (enhanced CD)
- "Blessings from Jesus" activity page, 1 per kid

Prompt kids to draw a picture in their journals of one of the things Jesus taught about how believers should live. If kids need ideas, suggest they draw a picture of a person loving her enemies or forgiving someone who wronged her. Kids may review Matthew 5–7 in their Bibles for more ideas.

Say • *What did Jesus teach in His Sermon on the Mount? Jesus taught how believers should live.*

Invite kids to share prayer requests. Close the group in prayer, or allow a couple volunteers to close the group in prayer. As time allows, lead kids to complete the activity page "Blessings from Jesus."

Leader BIBLE STUDY

The Gospels record dozens of Jesus' parables. A parable is a story Jesus told to help people understand the kingdom of God. Each parable taught a lesson and revealed secrets of God's kingdom for those who would understand. (See Matt. 13:10-13.)

The parable of the sower would have resonated with those listening because they would have been familiar with the practice of sowing or planting seed. But the parable had a deeper meaning. It contained a lesson about God's Word and the responses of those who hear it.

In the parable, a sower's seeds fell in four different places. Some of the seeds fell along the path, where they were eaten by birds. Other seeds fell on rocky ground. Those seeds had no roots, so they withered in the sun. Other seeds fell among thorns, and they were choked out. Other seeds fell on good soil, and they produced a crop—a hundred, sixty, or thirty times what was planted.

After Jesus told the parable, He explained it to His disciples. The soil represents people's hearts, and the seed is the word about God's kingdom. The person whose heart is like the hard soil hears the good news about God, but he does not understand it or he rejects it. The person whose heart is like the rocky soil is quick to receive the truth, but when life gets hard, he falls away. The person whose heart is like the thorny soil cares more about the things of the world than the good news about God, and the seed cannot grow. The person whose heart is like the good soil hears the good news about God and receives it. He bears fruit, more than what was planted. In the life of a believer, the fruit of the Spirit (Gal. 5:22-23) is evident.

Jesus' lesson still holds true today. People respond in various ways to the gospel, and not everyone who hears the gospel believes it. As you prepare to teach the parable of the sower, pray for the kids you lead. Pray that God will give them receptive hearts so that they will hear, understand, and receive the good news about Jesus.

Older Kids BIBLE STUDY OVERVIEW

Session Title: Parable of the Sower
Bible Passage: Matthew 13:1-23; Mark 4:1-20; Luke 8:4-15
Big Picture Question: How do people respond to the gospel? Some
people believe the gospel and others reject the gospel.
Key Passage: Matthew 6:33
Unit Christ Connection: Jesus taught people that the kingdom of God had
come and that salvation is available to all.

Small Group Opening

Large Group Leader

Small Group Leader

The BIBLE STORY

Parable of the Sower
Matthew 13:1-23; Mark 4:1-20; Luke 8:4-15

Jesus traveled around from one town and village to another. In each place, He preached the good news about the kingdom of God. Crowds of people came to listen to Jesus' teaching. **One day, Jesus was sitting by the sea. So many people came to hear Him that Jesus got into a boat and sat down to teach. The crowds stood on the shore to listen.**

Jesus used parables to teach the people. A parable is a story Jesus told to help people understand the kingdom of God. **Jesus told them a parable about a sower. He compared sharing the truth about Jesus to a man planting seeds in a field.**

Jesus said, **"Think about this. A sower went out to plant seeds in an area of ground. As he was planting, some seeds fell along the path. Soon, the birds came and ate up the seeds from the path. Other seeds fell on rocky ground where there wasn't much soil. The seeds sprouted quickly, but they did not have any roots because the soil was shallow. When the sun came up, the plants withered. Other seeds fell among thorns. The thorns grew, and they stopped the seeds from growing. But some of the seeds fell on good ground. Those seeds grew and produced a crop, more than what was planted!"**

Jesus' disciples came up to Him and **asked, "Why do You use parables to teach the people?"**

Jesus answered, "Not everyone will understand the truth about God's kingdom. I speak to them in parables because even though they look and hear, they do not see or understand. The prophet Isaiah wrote that this would happen." Jesus said that God had blessed the disciples with the ability to see and understand.

Then Jesus explained the parable to them. He said, "Some people hear the truth about God's kingdom, but they don't understand it. The evil one comes and takes away what was planted in their hearts. **Those people are like the seeds that fell on the path.**

"Some people hear the truth about God's kingdom, and they are happy to accept it. But when hard times come because of the truth,

they give up. **Those people are like the seeds that fell on rocky ground.**

"**Some people hear the truth about God's kingdom, but they worry about this life and they love money too much.** The truth cannot grow. **Those people are like the seeds that fell among thorns.**

"**But some people hear the truth about God's kingdom, and they understand it.** They accept the truth, and it grows in their lives. **Those people are like the seeds that fell on good ground.** Those seeds produce a crop, more than what was planted."

Christ Connection: Not everyone believes the truth about Jesus. Some don't understand it, some believe in Jesus for selfish reasons, and some only want part of Jesus because they love other things more. But those who hear the gospel and understand who Jesus is will become like Jesus and share His good news with others.

Small Group OPENING

Session Title: Parable of the Sower
Bible Passage: Matthew 13:1-23; Mark 4:1-20; Luke 8:4-15
Big Picture Question: How do people respond to the gospel? Some people believe the gospel and others reject the gospel.
Key Passage: Matthew 6:33
Unit Christ Connection: Jesus taught people that the kingdom of God had come and that salvation is available to all.

Welcome time

Greet each kid as he or she arrives. Use this time to collect the offering, fill out attendance sheets, and help new kids connect to your group.

Ask kids if they have ever planted something. Choose a few volunteers to respond. What did they plant? Did it grow? What did it need to grow? (*water, sunlight, warm temperature, and so forth*)

Activity page (5 minutes)

- "What's Growing?" activity page, 1 per kid
- crayons, colored pencils, or markers

Provide crayons, colored pencils, or markers for kids to complete the "What's Growing?" activity page. Point out the markers in the soil and encourage kids to draw what they think each seed might grow into.

Say • Today we are going to hear a story from the Bible that Jesus told about a man who planted seeds in a field. Jesus taught an important lesson about what happened to the seeds.

Session starter (10 minutes)

Option 1: To tell the truth
Direct kids to sit on the floor. Choose one volunteer to stand

in front of the group. Explain that the volunteer will tell the group three things about herself. Two of the statements will be true, and one of the statements will be false.

Invite kids to guess which statement is false. Then prompt the volunteer to reveal if the kids are correct. Choose another volunteer to give three statements and repeat the game as time allows.

Say • How do you know the truth when you hear it? Has anyone ever told you the truth about something and you didn't believe it? In today's Bible story, Jesus talked about how people respond to hearing the truth of the gospel.

Option 2: Seed swap

• beans or large seeds, 12 per kid
• ziplock bags

Give each kid a ziplock bag containing 12 beans or large seeds. Invite kids to move around the room and play in pairs. When a kid finds a partner, one player should reach into his bag and grab a handful of seeds and hold them in his fist. The other player will say "odd" or "even." The first player will count the seeds in his hand. If the second player guessed correctly—if the number of seeds is odd or even— he gets to keep the first player's seeds.

Play again with the second player grabbing seeds. Then guide kids to find new partners. Allow kids to play for several minutes. The goal is to have the most seeds in your bag when time is up.

Say • Today's Bible story is a parable, or a story that Jesus told to help people understand things about God's kingdom. Jesus' story was about a sower—a man who planted seeds in a field. Jesus used this story to teach His followers an important lesson.

Transition to large group

Jesus Preached

Large Group LEADER

Session Title: Parable of the Sower
Bible Passage: Matthew 13:1-23; Mark 4:1-20; Luke 8:4-15
Big Picture Question: How do people respond to the gospel? Some people believe the gospel and others reject the gospel.
Key Passage: Matthew 6:33
Unit Christ Connection: Jesus taught people that the kingdom of God had come and that salvation is available to all.

Countdown

• countdown video

Show the countdown video as your kids arrive, and set it to end as large group time begins.

Introduce the session (2 minutes)

• fishing pole
• Bible

[Large Group Leader enters with a fishing pole and Bible.]
Leader • Hello! It's so good to see you again. I'm [*your name*]. I was just heading out to my favorite fishing spot to fish and read the Bible. Come with me! Today I'm going to read another story that Jesus taught. Do you remember what we learned last time? Let's check out the timeline map to review.

Timeline map (2 minutes)

• Timeline Map

Use the timeline map to point out and review the previous Bible story, "The Sermon on the Mount."
Leader • Last time we learned about a sermon Jesus taught while He sat on a mountainside. ***What did Jesus teach in His Sermon on the Mount? Jesus taught how believers should live.*** Remember that Jesus said that believers should love their enemies and forgive others. That can be hard to do sometimes, but God loved us when we were

His enemies. We sinned and disobeyed Him, but God sent Jesus to rescue us from sin. When we trust in Jesus as Lord and Savior, God forgives our sin.

Big picture question (1 minute)

Leader •This week's Bible story is called "Parable of the Sower." Who can tell me what a *parable* is? (*A parable is a story Jesus told to help people understand the kingdom of God.*) With this parable, Jesus taught about how people respond to the gospel. That's our big picture question: ***How do people respond to the gospel?*** Listen to the Bible story to see if you can figure out the answer.

Tell the Bible story (10 minutes)

- "Parable of the Sower" video
- Bibles, 1 per kid
- Bible Story Picture Slide or Poster
- Big Picture Question Slide or Poster

Open your Bible to Matthew 13:1-23; Mark 4:1-20; or Luke 8:4-15. Tell the Bible story in your own words or show the Bible story video "Parable of the Sower."

Leader •The Gospels—Matthew, Mark, Luke, and John—record many parables that Jesus told. One day, Jesus told a simple story about a man planting seeds in a field. The man tossed the seeds onto the ground, and they fell in four different places.

The first seeds fell along the path. They sat on top of the ground, so the birds came and ate the seeds.

The next seeds fell on rocky ground. The soil was shallow, so when the seeds sprouted, they didn't have any roots. The sun came out and the plants dried up and died.

The next seeds fells among the weeds and thorns. The seeds couldn't grow because the thorns choked them; the weeds used up all the water and nutrients the seeds needed.

Finally, some of the seeds fell on good soil. These seeds had everything they needed to grow. They were strong and healthy, and when they grew, they made grain, much more than what was planted.

After Jesus told this story, His disciples asked Him to explain what the story meant. Jesus wasn't just telling a story about a farmer, after all. He was teaching something about God's kingdom.

Jesus said that the seeds were like people who hear the truth about God's kingdom. The seeds that fell along the path are like people who hear the truth and do not understand it. The seeds that fell on the rocky ground are like people who hear the truth and believe it right away, but when life gets hard, they stop believing.

The seeds that fell among the thorns are like people who hear the truth, but they have a hard time believing because they worry about life instead of trusting God. But the seeds that fell on the good soil are like people who hear the truth and believe it. The truth changes their hearts, and they grow to know and love Jesus.

How do people respond to the gospel? Some people believe the gospel and others reject the gospel. That's our big picture question and answer. Say it with me. *How do people respond to the gospel? Some people believe the gospel and others reject the gospel.*
Prompt kids to think about how they respond to the gospel.

Do they believe the good news about Jesus? Do they have questions? Do they doubt Jesus when life is hard? Do they reject it? Explain that not everyone who hears the good news believes it. We can pray that God would change people's hearts so they would accept the good news about Jesus and be saved from their sin.

The Gospel: God's Plan for Me (optional)

• Bible

Using Scripture and the guide provided, explain to boys and girls how to become a Christian. Tell kids how they

can respond, and provide counselors to speak with each kid individually. Encourage boys and girls to ask their parents, small group leaders, or other adults any questions they may have about becoming a Christian.

Key passage (5 minutes)

• Key Passage Slide or Poster
• "Seek Ye First" song

Display the key passage poster and lead kids to read it aloud together. Then lead the girls to say the first half and the boys to say the second half.

Leader • In the Bible story today, we learned that one of the reasons people do not believe the gospel is because they worry too much about life. They do not trust God. What does this verse say about trusting God?

If we put God first and care about the things He cares about—like knowing and loving Jesus and telling others about Him—then we can trust God to take care of us.

Invite kids to share a few things they sometimes worry about in their lives. Then sing the song "Seek Ye First."

Discussion starter video (5 minutes)

• "Unit 27 Session 2" discussion starter video

Leader • Think about the best news you've ever heard. Did you believe it when you heard it? What if you had some good news that your friend refused to believe? Watch this.

Show the "Unit 27 Session 2" video.

Leader • It might seem silly to react to good news by doubting or rejecting it, but Jesus said that not everyone who hears the good news about Him will believe it.

Prompt kids to discuss what challenges they might face when telling their friends or family members about Jesus. Assure them that they can pray for people who reject the gospel, the good news about Jesus. God has the power to change people's hearts.

Sing (3 minutes)

• "We Are" song

Leader • The Bible says that people who do not know Jesus as Lord and Savior live in darkness. They don't believe the good news that Jesus came to rescue us from sin. Jesus said in His Sermon on the Mount that believers should be like lights in a world of darkness. We can shine our light by telling others the truth about Jesus. Let's sing about that now.

Lead boys and girls to sing together "We Are."

Prayer (2 minutes)

Leader • *How do people respond to the gospel? Some people believe the gospel and others reject the gospel.* Let's pray for people who do not believe the gospel, the good news about Jesus.

Lead the kids in prayer. Thank God for sending Jesus to save people from sin. Ask that God would change the hearts of people who reject Him so that they would believe the truth about Jesus and love Him—and by doing so that they would be saved.

Dismiss to small groups

The Gospel: God's Plan for Me

Ask kids if they have ever heard the word *gospel*. Clarify that the word *gospel* means "good news." It is the message about Christ, the kingdom of God, and salvation. Use the following guide to share the gospel with kids.

God rules. Explain to kids that the Bible tells us God created everything, and He is in charge of everything. Invite a volunteer to read Genesis 1:1 from the Bible. Read Revelation 4:11 or Colossians 1:16-17 aloud and explain what these verses mean.

We sinned. Tell kids that since the time of Adam and Eve, everyone has chosen to disobey God. (Romans 3:23) The Bible calls this sin. Because God is holy, God cannot be around sin. Sin separates us from God and deserves God's punishment of death. (Romans 6:23)

God provided. Choose a child to read John 3:16 aloud. Say that God sent His Son, Jesus, the perfect solution to our sin problem, to rescue us from the punishment we deserve. It's something we, as sinners, could never earn on our own. Jesus alone saves us. Read and explain Ephesians 2:8-9.

Jesus gives. Share with kids that Jesus lived a perfect life, died on the cross for our sins, and rose again. Because Jesus gave up His life for us, we can be welcomed into God's family for eternity. This is the best gift ever! Read Romans 5:8; 2 Corinthians 5:21; or 1 Peter 3:18.

We respond. Tell kids that they can respond to Jesus. Read Romans 10:9-10,13. Review these aspects of our response: Believe in your heart that Jesus alone saves you through what He's already done on the cross. Repent, turning from self and sin to Jesus. Tell God and others that your faith is in Jesus.

Offer to talk with any child who is interested in responding to Jesus.

Small Group LEADER

Session Title: Parable of the Sower
Bible Passage: Matthew 13:1-23; Mark 4:1-20; Luke 8:4-15
Big Picture Question: How do people respond to the gospel? Some
people believe the gospel and others reject the gospel.
Key Passage: Matthew 6:33
Unit Christ Connection: Jesus taught people that the kingdom of God had
come and that salvation is available to all.

Key passage activity (5 minutes)

- Key Passage Poster
- chalkboards or dry erase boards, 2
- chalk or markers

Review the key passage once or twice, and then cover the
key passage poster. Form two teams of kids. Guide each
team to line up single file. Position a chalkboard or dry
erase board across form each team. Give the first player in
each line a piece of chalk or a marker.

When you say go, the first player should run to the
chalkboard and write the first word of the key passage. She
should then run back to her team, pass the chalk to the next
player, and move to the end of the line. Teams should work
together, writing one word at a time, until they finish the
key passage. When a team finishes, the players should sit.

Say • Great job, everyone! Memorizing God's Word is so
helpful. When you start to worry about your life,
remember this Bible verse. God is faithful and good.

Bible story review & Bible skills (10 minutes)

- Bibles, 1 per kid
- Small Group Visual Pack
- sheets of paper, 4
- marker
- tape

Review the timeline in the small group visual pack. Provide
a Bible for each kid and guide them to find Matthew 13
in the Bible. Retell or review the Bible story in your own
words or use the bolded text of the Bible story script.

Invite kids to play a game of "Four Corners." Label four
pieces of paper A, B, C, and D, and hang one paper in each

corner of the room. Read the following review questions. After you read a set of multiple-choice answers, kids should move to the corner that corresponds with the correct answer. Reveal the answer, and then instruct kids to return to the center of the room to hear the next question.

1. Where did Jesus tell the parable about the sower? A. in the synagogue; B. on a mountain; C. in His house; D. in a boat by the sea (*D. in a boat by the sea; Matt. 13:1; Mark 4:1*)

2. What happened to the seeds on the path? A. The birds ate the seeds; B. The wind blew away the seeds; C. Travelers stepped on the seeds; D. The seeds withered in the sun. (*A. The birds ate the seeds; Matt. 13:4; Mark 4:4; Luke 8:5*)

3. What happened to the seeds on rocky ground? A. The seeds grew and produced a crop; B. The seeds grew quickly but withered in the sun; C. The birds ate the seeds; D. Wild donkeys ate the seeds. (*B. The seeds grew quickly but withered in the sun; Matt. 13:5-6; Mark 4:5-6; Luke 8:6*)

4. What happened to the seeds among the thorns? A. They grew and produced a crop; B. They grew quickly but withered in the sun; C. The thorns choked them; D. They grew like weeds. (*C. The thorns choked them; Matt. 13:7; Mark 4:7; Luke 8:7*)

5. What happened to the seeds on the good ground? A. They grew up and produced a crop, many times what was sown; B. They grew quickly but withered in the sun; C. They were washed away by the rain; D. They never grew. (*A. They grew and produced a crop, many times what was sown; Matt. 13:8; Mark 4:8; Luke 8:8*)

Guide kids to return to the center of the room to review the big picture question and answer. If you choose to review with boys and girls how to become a Christian, explain that kids are welcome to speak with you or another teacher if they have questions.

- **God rules.** God created and is in charge of everything. (Gen. 1:1; Rev. 4:11; Col. 1:16-17)
- **We sinned.** Since Adam and Eve, everyone has chosen to disobey God. (Rom. 3:23; 6:23)
- **God provided.** God sent His Son, Jesus, to rescue us from the punishment we deserve. (John 3:16; Eph. 2:8-9)
- **Jesus gives.** Jesus lived a perfect life, died on the cross for our sins, and rose again so we can be welcomed into God's family. (Rom. 5:8; 2 Cor. 5:21; 1 Pet. 3:18)
- **We respond.** Believe that Jesus alone saves you. Repent. Tell God that your faith is in Jesus. (Rom. 10:9-10,13)

· Gospel Plan Poster
(enhanced CD)

Activity choice (10 minutes)

Option 1: Share the good news

Use the gospel plan poster to review the gospel. Help kids begin to feel comfortable sharing the gospel with others. Ask the following questions:

1. Who rules? (*God rules. God created everything, and He is in charge of everything.*)
2. What did we do? (*We sinned. Sin separates us from God, and the punishment for sin is death.*)
3. Who provided? (*God provided. God sent Jesus to rescue us from the punishment we deserve.*)
4. Who gives? (*Jesus gives. Jesus gave up His life for us so we can live with God forever.*)

5. What do we do now? (*We respond. We can turn from our sin and turn to Jesus.*)

Say • Think about someone you can share the gospel with this week. Pray that he or she will respond to the good news about Jesus by believing in Him.

Option 2: Dirt pudding cups

- 1 package chocolate instant pudding
- 2 cups cold milk
- 8 ounces whipped topping
- 1¼ cups crushed chocolate cookies
- 10 worm-shaped chewy fruit snacks
- 10 small paper or plastic cups
- plastic spoons
- napkins
- Allergy Alert (enhanced CD)

Prepare the pudding cups prior to small group. The recipe makes 10 cups. Whisk together the pudding mix and milk in a large bowl. Let stand for five minutes. Stir in whipped topping and half of the crushed cookies. Spoon into 10 small cups and top with remaining crushed cookies. Refrigerate one hour. Top with a fruit snack before serving.

Serve a prepared pudding cup to each kid. Provide plastic spoons and napkins. As kids enjoy their snack, lead them to talk about the Bible story. Review the four types of soils and what they each represent.

Say • *How do people respond to the gospel? Some people believe the gospel and others reject the gospel.*

Journal and prayer (5 minutes)

- pencils
- journals
- Bibles
- Journal Page, 1 per kid (enhanced CD)
- "Four Soils" activity page, 1 per kid

Lead kids to think about how they have responded to the gospel. Encourage kids to write in their journals a *1, 2,* or *3* based on the following responses:

1. I'm not sure.
2. I am interested, but I have questions.
3. I believe the gospel and trust in Jesus as Lord and Savior.

Be available to speak with any kids who have questions about the gospel or about becoming a Christian. Invite kids to share prayer requests. Close the group in prayer, or allow a couple volunteers to close the group in prayer. As time allows, lead kids to complete the activity page "Four Soils."

Leader BIBLE STUDY

In Luke 19, Jesus went after Zacchaeus, a chief tax collector. Zacchaeus was not well liked, but his interaction with Jesus led him to repent of his wrongdoing. Jesus said to him, "The Son of Man has come to seek and to save the lost" (Luke 19:10).

Who is "the lost"? What does it mean to be lost? In Luke 15, Jesus told three parables to the crowd of tax collectors, sinners, Pharisees, and scribes. Jesus' teaching brought gospel truth to the tax collectors and sinners—those whose unrighteousness separated them from God—and to the Pharisees and scribes—those whose relied on their own righteous efforts for salvation.

The first two parables are similar. In one, a man loses a sheep. He leaves his flock to find the missing sheep, and he rejoices when it is found. In the second, a woman loses a silver coin. The woman carefully searches her home until she finds it. Then, she calls her neighbors and friends to celebrate with her. Heaven rejoices when even one sinner repents. Finally, Jesus told a parable about two sons. The younger son asked for his inheritance. He wasted his money on immoral living and decided to return to his father. Rather than rejecting his wayward son, the father embraced him. The older son, who had always been obedient to his father, reacted with anger.

As you read Luke 15, think about the crowd Jesus was speaking to. The focus is often placed on the younger son—the one with whom the tax collectors and sinners could identify—but Jesus also made a point about the older son. He was like the Pharisees and scribes, focused on his own morality and feeling entitled to his father's favor.

Jesus taught what God is like. He seeks sinners who have wandered far from Him, and He seeks sinners who try to earn salvation by their good works. As you teach, help kids understand that being lost means not knowing Jesus as Lord and Savior. God loves us, and He actively seeks sinners to bring them to Himself.

Older Kids BIBLE STUDY OVERVIEW

Session Title: Three Parables
Bible Passage: Luke 15
Big Picture Question: What does it mean to be lost? Being lost means not knowing Jesus as Lord and Savior.
Key Passage: Matthew 6:33
Unit Christ Connection: Jesus taught people that the kingdom of God had come and that salvation is available to all.

Small Group Opening

Large Group Leader

Small Group Leader

The BIBLE STORY

Three Parables
Luke 15

Tax collectors and sinners came to Jesus to listen to Him teach. The Pharisees and scribes complained. "This man welcomes sinners and eats with them!" they said. **So Jesus told them three parables to teach them about Himself.**

First, Jesus told a parable about a lost sheep. **Jesus said, "If a man has 100 sheep and loses one of them, what does he do? He leaves the 99 sheep in the open field and searches for the lost sheep until he finds it.** And when he finds it, he is happy! He carries the sheep on his shoulders and goes home. **Then he tells his friends and neighbors, 'Celebrate with me because I have found my lost sheep!'"**

Then Jesus said, "This is what heaven is like, only there is more joy in heaven when one sinner repents and turns back to God than when 99 righteous people don't need to repent."

The next parable was about a lost coin. **Jesus said, "If a woman has 10 silver coins and loses one of them, what does she do? She lights a lamp, sweeps the house, and searches carefully until she finds it!** And when she finds it, **she calls her friends and neighbors together and says, 'Celebrate with me! I have found my lost coin!'"**

Then Jesus said, "This is what heaven is like. God's angels celebrate when one sinner repents and turns back to God."

Finally, Jesus told a parable about a lost son. Jesus said, "A man had two sons. The younger son told his father, 'Father, give me my inheritance today.' So the father gave his son his share. A few days later, **the younger son left home.** He took everything he had and went to a distant country. **He wasted his money and lived foolishly. When he had nothing left,** there was a famine in the country. The people who lived there did not have enough food. **The son got a job feeding pigs. The son was hungry,** and he wished he could eat the food the pigs were eating, but no one gave him any food.

"The younger son realized he had been foolish. He thought of the men who worked for his father. They had more than enough food, yet he was dying of hunger. **The son made a plan. He would go back to his father and admit he was wrong. He would ask to work for the father like the hired men.**

"So the younger son headed home. He was still a long way away when his father saw him coming. His father ran to him and threw his arms around his son's neck and kissed him. The son began to apologize to his father.** 'I have sinned against God and was wrong to you,' he said. 'I am not worthy to be called your son.'

"**But the father told his servants,** 'Hurry! Bring out the best clothes and put it on him. Put a ring on his finger and sandals on his feet. Then bring the fattened calf and kill it. **Let's celebrate with a feast! This son of mine was lost, and now he is found!'** So they began to celebrate.

"**At this time, the older son came from the fields** and heard music and dancing at the house. **He asked one of the servants what was going on.**

"'**Your brother is here,' the servant said. 'Your father is celebrating** because he is home safe and sound.'

"**The older brother was angry! He refused to go to the feast. The father** met him and **asked him to come inside. 'Look!' the older brother said.** 'I have worked hard for you for years! **I never disobeyed you! But you never even gave me a goat to celebrate with my friends.** But when this son of yours—who has wasted your money—comes home, you kill the fattened calf for him!'

"'**Son,' the father said, 'everything I have is yours. But we had to celebrate and be happy. Your brother was lost and is found.'**"

Christ Connection: A shepherd was seeking his sheep, a woman was seeking her coin, and a father was seeking his prodigal son. Jesus told these parables to teach about Himself. As Savior, Jesus seeks sinners. He paid the ultimate price—His own life—to save people from sin.

Small Group OPENING

Session Title: Three Parables
Bible Passage: Luke 15
Big Picture Question: What does it mean to be lost? Being lost means not knowing Jesus as Lord and Savior.
Key Passage: Matthew 6:33
Unit Christ Connection: Jesus taught people that the kingdom of God had come and that salvation is available to all.

Welcome time

Greet each kid as he or she arrives. Use this time to collect the offering, fill out attendance sheets, and help new kids connect to your group.

Invite one or two kids to share about a time they made a choice and then realized it was the wrong choice. How did they feel? What did they do?

Activity page (5 minutes)

• "Lost and Found" activity page, 1 per kid
• pencils

Distribute the "Lost and Found" activity page to kids. Allow kids to work individually or in pairs to carefully search the picture. Explain that each person in the picture has lost something. Challenge boys and girls to find and circle the lost items.

Say • When we lose something, we want to find it. The Bible says that Jesus came into the world to seek and save people who are lost. (Luke 19:10) We'll find out more about what that means in today's Bible story.

Session starter (10 minutes)

Option 1: Things in common
Challenge kids to listen carefully to the items you list to

figure out what they have in common. When a kid thinks he knows the answer, he should raise his hand. After several kids' hands are raised, call on someone to answer. If he is correct, begin again with a new category. If he is incorrect, continue naming items in the category.

Play several rounds, using the following suggestions as well as your own categories:

1. banana, watermelon, lemon, kiwi (*fruits*)
2. basketball, hockey, tennis, lacrosse (*sports*)
3. tea, milk, water, lemonade (*beverages*)
4. lost coin, lost sheep, lost son (*parables*)

Say • Today we are going to hear a Bible story about three parables Jesus told. These parables are about a lost coin, a lost sheep, and a lost son.

Option 2: Seek and find

• large coin
• toy sheep

Form two teams of kids. Assign the sheep to one team and the coin to the other. Choose one volunteer from each team to be a seeker. Send the seekers out of the room with an adult leader or ask them to cover their eyes.

Hide the large coin and the toy sheep in separate places in the room. Allow the teams to see where you hide the items. Call the seekers back. Explain that the sheep team should say "baa" loudly or softly to indicate how close the seeker is to the sheep. The coin team should say "cha-ching" loudly or softly to help the seeker find the coin.

Invite the seekers to begin seeking. If time allows, play another round after seekers find the items.

Say • In today's Bible story, Jesus told about three things that were lost: a lost coin, a lost sheep, and a lost son.

Transition to large group

Large Group LEADER

Session Title: Three Parables
Bible Passage: Luke 15
Big Picture Question: What does it mean to be lost? Being lost means not knowing Jesus as Lord and Savior.
Key Passage: Matthew 6:33
Unit Christ Connection: Jesus taught people that the kingdom of God had come and that salvation is available to all.

Countdown

• countdown video

Show the countdown video as your kids arrive, and set it to end as large group time begins.

Introduce the session (2 minutes)

• sunglasses
• beach towel
• Bible

[Large Group Leader enters wearing sunglasses. Leader carries a beach towel and a Bible.]

Leader • Hi! I'm so glad you're here. I'm [*your name*]. Are you ready to get started with today's Bible study? I was just heading out with my beach towel to find a warm spot near the lake to sit and read God's Word. This is the last time I'll see you to study about the things Jesus preached, but I've had such a great time! Before we get started with today's story, let's review what we learned the last couple of times we met.

Timeline map (2 minutes)

• Timeline Map

Use the timeline map to point out and review the previous Bible stories, "The Sermon on the Mount" and "Parable of the Sower."

Leader • Do you remember "The Sermon on the Mount"? ***What did Jesus teach in His Sermon on the Mount?***

Jesus taught how believers should live.

Then Jesus told a parable, or story, about a man planting seeds in a field. Jesus used this story to teach people about how people respond to the gospel, the good news about Him. *How do people respond to the gospel? Some people believe the gospel and others reject the gospel.*

Big picture question (1 minute)

Leader • Today's Bible story is called "Three Parables." Well, that makes sense because it's about three parables Jesus told about a lost sheep, a lost coin, and a lost son.

As you listen to the Bible story, don't forget to listen to figure out the answer to our big picture question. This week's big picture question is, *What does it mean to be lost?* That's an interesting question.

Tell the Bible story (10 minutes)

Open your Bible to Luke 15 and tell the Bible story in your own words, or show the Bible story video "Three Parables."

Leader • What was Jesus' first parable about? (*a lost sheep*) The man who lost his sheep left behind his flock of 99 sheep to find the sheep that was lost. When he found the sheep, he celebrated! He was so happy. Jesus said that this is what heaven is like. The angels celebrate when someone who is lost turns from their sin and turns to God.

What does it mean to be lost? Being lost means not knowing Jesus as Lord and Savior. Yes! That's our big picture question and answer. Say it with me. *What does it mean to be lost? Being lost means not knowing Jesus as Lord and Savior.*

Jesus' second parable was about a woman who lost a coin. She cleaned and searched her house until she found

- "Three Parables" video
- Bibles, 1 per kid
- Bible Story Picture Slide or Poster
- Big Picture Question Slide or Poster

the coin. When she found it, she celebrated! Jesus said that this is what heaven is like. The angels celebrate when someone who is lost turns from their sin and turns to God.

Jesus' third parable was about a son who left his father's home. He went to another country and wasted all his money. The son realized he had made bad choices, and he decided to go back home to his father. Maybe his father would give him a job as a servant. At least he would have food to eat and a roof over his head.

When the son went home, what did the father do? Was the father angry at him for being foolish? No! The father saw his son coming, and he ran to him! He gave him a big hug and a kiss, and he threw a party! The father was so happy to have his son home!

Did you know that's what God is like? We are foolish when we sin and disobey God, but God wants us to turn back to Him. He will not be angry when we tell Him we are sorry; He will be happy!

That's not the end of the story, though. The son had an older brother. The brother was angry that the father celebrated when the younger son came home. The older brother had always obeyed the father, and he didn't think it was fair for the father to throw a party for the younger son. Jesus told this story because the Pharisees and other religious leaders were like the older brother. They tried hard to obey God's laws, and they didn't think Jesus should be friends with people who do bad things. The good news is that Jesus *is* friends with sinners! We are all sinners, and Jesus wants us to trust in Him.

The Gospel: God's Plan for Me (optional)

• Bible

Using Scripture and the guide provided, explain to boys and girls how to become a Christian. Tell kids how they

can respond, and provide counselors to speak with each kid individually. Guide counselors to use open-ended questions to allow kids to determine the direction of the conversation.

Encourage boys and girls to ask their parents, small group leaders, or other adults any questions they may have about becoming a Christian.

Key passage (5 minutes)

• Key Passage Slide or Poster
• "Seek Ye First" song

Leader • Can anyone say our key passage from memory? Invite any kids who have memorized the key passage to recite it aloud. Then display the key passage poster. Remind kids that Jesus said these words in His Sermon on the Mount. Jesus said that we can trust God to take care of us.

Choose a volunteer or two to lead the group in singing the key passage song, "Seek Ye First."

Discussion starter video (5 minutes)

• "Unit 27 Session 3" discussion starter video

Leader • Have you ever been physically lost, like in a crowd? Maybe you couldn't find your friends or one of your parents. Watch this video.
Show the "Unit 27 Session 3" video. Then invite kids to share any stories they have about being lost. Where were they? How did they feel? What did they do?

Leader • Being lost is a scary feeling! Did you know that many people in the world are lost and don't even know it? They may not be physically lost, but they are spiritually lost. *What does it mean to be lost? Being lost means not knowing Jesus as Lord and Savior.*

People who don't know Jesus as Lord and Savior are called *lost* because they can't find their way to God. Their sin separates them from God, and the only way to get to God is to believe in Jesus.

Sing (3 minutes)

• "We Are" song

Leader •You know, if I were physically lost and unable to find my way, I would want someone to show me the way. Do you remember what Jesus said about believers in His Sermon on the Mount? He said that believers are like lights in a dark world. You can help people who are lost find their way by telling them about Jesus. Let's sing our theme song together.

Lead boys and girls to sing "We Are."

Prayer (2 minutes)

Leader •Let's pray. Father God, forgive us for the times we are foolish like the younger son, turning away from You and making bad choices. Thank You for sending Jesus to rescue us from our sins. Without Jesus, we are lost, but the Bible says in Luke 19:10 that Jesus came to seek and save the lost. We know that salvation is a gift from You; we can never do anything to earn it.

Help us be lights in a dark world full of people who do not know and love you. Give us courage to tell others the good news about Jesus. We want to celebrate when You save people from their sins. We love You. Amen.

Dismiss to small groups

The Gospel: God's Plan for Me

Ask kids if they have ever heard the word *gospel*. Clarify that the word *gospel* means "good news." It is the message about Christ, the kingdom of God, and salvation. Use the following guide to share the gospel with kids.

God rules. Explain to kids that the Bible tells us God created everything, and He is in charge of everything. Invite a volunteer to read Genesis 1:1 from the Bible. Read Revelation 4:11 or Colossians 1:16-17 aloud and explain what these verses mean.

We sinned. Tell kids that since the time of Adam and Eve, everyone has chosen to disobey God. (Romans 3:23) The Bible calls this sin. Because God is holy, God cannot be around sin. Sin separates us from God and deserves God's punishment of death. (Romans 6:23)

God provided. Choose a child to read John 3:16 aloud. Say that God sent His Son, Jesus, the perfect solution to our sin problem, to rescue us from the punishment we deserve. It's something we, as sinners, could never earn on our own. Jesus alone saves us. Read and explain Ephesians 2:8-9.

Jesus gives. Share with kids that Jesus lived a perfect life, died on the cross for our sins, and rose again. Because Jesus gave up His life for us, we can be welcomed into God's family for eternity. This is the best gift ever! Read Romans 5:8; 2 Corinthians 5:21; or 1 Peter 3:18.

We respond. Tell kids that they can respond to Jesus. Read Romans 10:9-10,13. Review these aspects of our response: Believe in your heart that Jesus alone saves you through what He's already done on the cross. Repent, turning from self and sin to Jesus. Tell God and others that your faith is in Jesus.

Offer to talk with any child who is interested in responding to Jesus.

Small Group LEADER

Session Title: Three Parables
Bible Passage: Luke 15
Big Picture Question: What does it mean to be lost? Being lost means not knowing Jesus as Lord and Savior.
Key Passage: Matthew 6:33
Unit Christ Connection: Jesus taught people that the kingdom of God had come and that salvation is available to all.

Key passage activity (5 minutes)

• Key Passage Poster
• strips of paper
• glue or stapler
• marker

Write the words of the key passage on separate strips of paper. If your group is large, make more than one set and direct kids to work in small groups. Give kids a set of key passage strips. Challenge them to put the words in order.

When kids finish, show the key passage poster to check their work. Then allow kids to roll and glue or staple the strips to make a paper chain. Lead the group to say the key passage aloud together.

Say • Great work, everyone. If you haven't memorized Matthew 6:33, I hope you'll keep working on it.

Bible story review & Bible skills (10 minutes)

• Bibles, 1 per kid
• Small Group Visual Pack
• craft sticks
• marker

Provide a Bible for each kid and instruct kids to stand. Guide them to find Luke 15 in the Bible. When a kid has located the book, she may sit down. Assist any kids who need help.

Review the timeline in the small group visual pack. Retell or review the Bible story in your own words or use the bolded text of the Bible story script.

Write each child's name on a craft stick. Ask the following review questions. Pull a craft stick and call on the kid whose name you pulled to answer the question. When a kid gives an answer, provide the Scripture reference and encourage kids to read the verse to check the answer.

1. ***What does it mean to be lost? Being lost means not knowing Jesus as Lord and Savior.***

2. Why were the religious leaders upset with Jesus? (*Jesus was friends with sinners, Luke 15:2*)

3. What animal did Jesus tell a parable about? (*sheep, Luke 15:3-6*)

4. What did the woman lose in her house? (*a coin, Luke 15:8*)

5. Which son took his inheritance and left home? (*the younger son, Luke 15:12-13*)

6. What work did the younger son do in a distant country? (*He fed pigs, Luke 15:15*)

7. How did the father react when he saw his son coming home? (*He ran to him, threw his arms around his son's neck, and kissed him; Luke 15:20*)

8. What did the father do to celebrate the younger brother's return? (*He threw a party, Luke 15:22-24*)

9. How did the older brother react when he heard the younger brother was home? (*He was angry, Luke 15:28*)

10. Who seeks after sinners and saves them? (*Jesus, Luke 19:10*)

If you choose to review with boys and girls how to become a Christian, explain that kids are welcome to speak with you or another teacher if they have questions.

- **God rules.** God created and is in charge of everything. (Gen. 1:1; Rev. 4:11; Col. 1:16-17)
- **We sinned.** Since Adam and Eve, everyone has chosen to disobey God. (Rom. 3:23; 6:23)
- **God provided.** God sent His Son, Jesus, to rescue

us from the punishment we deserve. (John 3:16; Eph. 2:8-9)

- **Jesus gives.** Jesus lived a perfect life, died on the cross for our sins, and rose again so we can be welcomed into God's family. (Rom. 5:8; 2 Cor. 5:21; 1 Pet. 3:18)

- **We respond.** Believe that Jesus alone saves you. Repent. Tell God that your faith is in Jesus. (Rom. 10:9-10,13)

Activity choice (10 minutes)

• play dough

Option 1: Lost items

Give each kid a lump of play dough. Invite kids to form items related to the Bible story: a sheep, a coin, or a son.

As kids work, allow them to retell the parable for the object they chose to shape. Remind kids that Jesus told these parables to teach about Himself. He gave up His own life to save people from sin.

Say •*What does it mean to be lost? Being lost means not knowing Jesus as Lord and Savior.*

Option 2: Roll and review

• "Review Cube" (enhanced CD)
• scissors
• glue or tape

Print, cut out, and assemble the review cube. Invite kids to take turns tossing the cube. For the picture that lands faceup, the kid who tossed the cube should state one thing she remembers about that Bible story. Then allow another kid to take a turn. If someone rolls a story already discussed, encourage him to recall another detail. If kids need help, lead them to find in the Bible the passage listed on the cube and review the Bible story. Challenge kids to recall the big picture question and answer from each story:

1. *Why do we need to be born again? Because of sin we are spiritually dead, but Jesus came to give*

us new life. ("Jesus Met Nicodemus")

2. *What does Jesus offer? Jesus offers eternal life.* ("Jesus Met a Samaritan Woman")

3. *How can we show we are thankful to Jesus? We can serve Jesus and live for Him.* ("Jesus Healed Peter's Mother-in-Law")

4. *Who can take away our sin? Jesus can and wants to cleanse us from sin.* ("Jesus Cleansed a Leper")

5. *What did Jesus teach in His Sermon on the Mount? Jesus taught how believers should live.* ("Sermon on the Mount")

6. *What does it mean to be lost? Being lost means not knowing Jesus as Lord and Savior.* ("Three Parables")

Say • All these Bible stories are about things Jesus taught or people Jesus healed. Jesus did many wonderful things while He was on earth, but what was His main purpose for coming to earth? (*God sent Jesus to earth to rescue people from their sins.*) That's good news!

Journal and prayer (5 minutes)

- pencils
- journals
- Bibles
- Journal Page, 1 per kid (enhanced CD)
- "Three Parables" activity page, 1 per kid

Prompt kids to think of someone they know who is lost—someone who doesn't know Jesus as Lord and Savior. Encourage them to write a short prayer in their journals, asking God for the opportunity to tell that person the good news about Jesus. If any kids in your group are unbelievers, invite them to pray that God would help them believe the truth about His Son, Jesus.

Invite kids to share prayer requests. Close the group in prayer, or allow a couple volunteers to close the group in prayer. As time allows, lead kids to complete the activity page "Three Parables."

How Smaller Churches Can Reach Children

Sometimes being a small church can seem like a large problem. We have good relationships with the people, but we can't do all the ministries we want—those we see flourishing in larger churches. In fact, sometimes we limit ourselves by the feeling of limitations. How small is small when it comes to ministering to children?

Small is a relative term. We are a small church if we are smaller than other churches or if we are not as large as we expect to become. Churches with an average attendance of 30, 50, 100, or 200, or more can be considered "small" if they want to become larger. And as long as there are unreached children, there is room to grow.

Why worry about it?

Children need nurturing and equipping to become joyful, purposeful adults who see his or her spiritual life as a first priority. Their futures and the futures of our churches depend on success in ministering to these children and their families now. Yet in small churches, quality preschool and children's ministry is often the area that gets the least attention.

How do you start a ministry for children?

Begin by deciding what you want to accomplish in the next 6 to 12 months. Then, in everything you do, keep your vision in focus. We want kids to have a great time, and we want them to learn. But ultimately, we want to see children and families walking with God as a result of where we spend our time and efforts.

Here are some tips on creating a healthy children's ministry in your church.

➤ Be ready to accept God's call on your own life and enlist prayer warriors.

➤ Prepare for the families who will

come to your church. Are there enough teachers and space for the growth that will come?

➤ Begin building relationships with families and children.
➤ Plan family-gathering activities.
➤ Plan time just for kids.

We want kids to have a great time, and we want them to learn. But ultimately, we want to see children and families walking with God as a result of where we spend our time and efforts.

What are the obstacles and how do we overcome them?

Obstacle 1: No Passions

Solution: You can become that person of passion. Perhaps this is your invitation to join God in the work He wants you to do with the children in your community.

Steps to take:
➤ Pray for yourself and for the children in your church and community.
➤ Enlist prayer warriors who will faithfully pray for you and this

ministry.
➤ Volunteer to fill this gap.
➤ Look for seminars that will help. Check with LifeWay or your state office for opportunities.
➤ Browse *www.lifeway.com/kids* for articles and resources that will help.
➤ Find a mentor who will offer advice and encouragement. Many state conventions have consultants whose jobs are to make you successful. They may suggest someone nearby who can help.

Obstacle 2: No Teachers

Solution: Ask others to join you for short-term projects.

Steps to take:
➤ Start with parents who have a commitment to their children and may be willing to help with some of the activities.
➤ Look at the hobbies, careers, and general skills of church members. Combine these with simple Bible study lessons and you can reach more than the children in your church.
➤ Watch and see which adults attract children. They will be smiling, talking, and stooping down to the child's eye level.

- Invite prospective adult volunteers to help you assist the children at the next event.
- Look around for people on the fringe. My friends call me a "vacuum" because I'm always "sucking" them into some activity. It works!

Obstacle 3: No Money

Solution: As you plan, write down everything you need. Even if you intend to provide it yourself. That will make next year's planning easier.

Steps to take:
- Submit a budget to the finance committee this summer for next year's activities. Even if they are unable to allocate money, it will help them understand what is needed.
- Plan some no-cost events. Does someone in your church have a large yard that would make a good kickball field? Also, many community events are free and can be attended as a group.
- Expect some activities to be self-paying events, but be aware of those who need financial assistance.
- Look for benefactors and scholarship providers. Ask an adult Sunday School class or those on the finance committee for help.

Obstacle 4: No Kids

Solution: Ministry has a cost! 1 Corinthians 9:15-27 will challenge you to pay the cost to build relationships—not potential converts. That's a time cost for you.

Steps to take:
- Look for places to develop relationships with families.
- Go to a ball game or another activity where you will meet families.
- Develop a business-card-sized promo piece and ask members to give them to neighbors and friends. Lead the church to host an event for the whole town where you might meet families.
- Brainstorm what talents your church members have and see if they can be used to meet families.
- Hold an event on neutral ground. A local park can be less threatening than a church building.
- Ask kids to bring friends. Then ask those friends to bring friends.

Obstacle 5: No Ideas

Solution: Use the Internet, the library, and friends to come up with fresh ideas. Then watch for teachable moments when you can weave Bible truths into the conversation while engaged in a "non-spiritual" activity.

Steps to take:
➤ Plan for holidays and seasons. Christmas and Easter are easy, but a President's Day costume party might be fun, too.
➤ Choose a theme for a central focus, such as a basketball or gardening party. Choose an appropriate lesson and adapt it to the situation.
➤ Educational field trips such as a museum or zoo with draw children and parents. Historical events or a literature theme can be fun, too.

➤ Watch the community calendar and ask yourself, "How can I use this to enhance my children's ministry?"
➤ Don't forget that children love to have fun together while serving others.

So ... get started!

➤ Accept God's call on your life and enlist prayer warriors.
➤ Get space and teachers ready for the families who will come to your church.
➤ Set a focus for the next 6 to 12 months of your ministry.
➤ Plan for the children you already have in church.
➤ Begin looking for relationships with new families and children.

Adapted from an article posted on *www.lifeway.com.*

Teaching Kids the Harmony of the Gospels

In this volume of *The Gospel Project*, you may notice we've cited more than one Gospel as the primary Scripture reference for a story. We cite more than one passage because we are moving chronologically through the story of the Bible, and therefore, we seek to harmonize the Gospels by enjoying the different perspectives of Matthew, Mark, Luke, and John on a particular event.

But what do you do if some of the kids in your group read the story from one Gospel, while other kids read the story from another Gospel? They may notice slight differences between the accounts.

Take the story of the Gadarene demoniac as an example. In Mark and Luke's accounts, Jesus encounters a demon-possessed man who comes out from among the tombs. But the Gospel of Matthew tells us there were actually two demon-possessed men. One could also note how the Gospel writers arrange events according to geography, and sometimes the chronology of accounts is different. Why are there differences? And how should we respond?

Here are some principles for discussing these issues with the kids in your group:

1. We believe the Bible is God's Word to us, and therefore, it is true.

It's important to affirm our trust in God and His Word. Because we believe God is good and true, we believe His Word to be truth without any mixture of error. Our belief in the inspiration and inerrancy of Scripture is grounded in our understanding of God's character. God does not lie. His Word does not contain errors.

2. God shaped His Word through the personalities of the Bible's authors.

God is not the Bible's only author. In grace, He chose to

ork through human writers, carrying them along by His Spirit and inspiring their words as they wrote. For this reason, the Bible is gloriously diverse. Paul's letters sound different than Peter's. John's Gospel is distinct from Luke's. God did not override the personalities of the apostles when they wrote the Gospels. He worked through them, and in the process, He gave us a multifaceted portrayal of the Son of God.

3. The Gospel writers tell us the truth about Jesus.

Little differences between the Gospel accounts shouldn't be blown out of proportion. The Gospel writers are remarkably united on the story of Jesus.

They affirm that Jesus is God's Son, sent to bring about the kingdom of God through His perfect life, substitutionary death, and victorious resurrection. The Gospels are invaluable to us because they are eyewitness accounts of Christ's majesty, written down within a generation of Jesus' life, in order to edify God's people and evangelize those who do not yet believe.

4. The Gospel writers tell us the truth about Jesus—differently.

The Gospel writers are united in their view of Jesus, and yet each writer wants to express the truth about Jesus differently. Mark is action-packed, focusing more

on Jesus' miracles than on Jesus' teaching. Matthew constantly quotes from the Old Testament to show us how Jesus fulfills the promise of the long-awaited King. Luke loves parables, and he emphasizes Jesus' care for the poor and oppressed. John lets us hear Jesus' long speeches about His relationship to the Father, and the Father's love for the world.

The Gospel writers all tell the truth about Jesus, but they tell the truth in different ways, drawing out different details. They felt free to rearrange chronology, shape their storytelling through the use of geography, or draw out other details.

In the example mentioned earlier, Mark and Luke summarize the story about one Gadarene demoniac. Matthew, who would've been present at the original occasion, wants us to know that there were, in fact, two. Mark and Luke never deny what Matthew says; they simply focus their attention on the better-known of the two men.

I'm thankful God gave us four portraits of Jesus, not just one. If you told four painters to sit down at a canvas and replicate a sunset, you'd find that each painter notices different things and draws attention to them in their painting. We wouldn't throw out the paintings, saying, *These aren't the same!* Instead, we'd marvel at the beauty of the different details and rejoice in the various perspectives at play. Encourage the kids in your group to not stumble over these differences, but to see them as complementary perspectives.

Trevin Wax is managing editor of *The Gospel Project* for Kids.